"Thou Shalt ...

Thou Shalt Not..."

IN THIS READABLE and remarkably interesting volume, one of today's leading Biblical scholars re-tells the story—in the light of modern knowledge—of Moses and the migration of the Hebrews from Egypt, and analyzes the meaning of the Ten Commandments throughout the course of history from early times to the present day.

Dr. Davies, minister of All Souls Church, Washington, D. C., and author of many religious volumes, presents a vivid picture of Old Testament leadership, the painful struggles of the Hebrew people against the Pharaoh in Egypt, the temptations offered by idol worshippers after their flight, and the final establishment of their kingdom in the Promised Land.

Now many people, stimulated by films, editorials, and the renewed, world-wide interest in religion, are turning toward the Scriptures. This timely volume is at once an invaluable aid to understanding the *Decalogue* and a fascinating account of the origin of the moral foundation of the Jewish and Christian faiths.

SIGNET KEY and MENTOR
Books of Interest

THE MEANING OF THE DEAD SEA SCROLLS
by A. Powell Davies

A fascinating interpretation of one of the most important archaeological discoveries of recent times, ancient documents which revolutionize religious teachings and beliefs. (#Ks339—35¢)

THE HOLY BIBLE In Brief
edited and arranged by James Reeves

The basic story of the Old and New Testaments told as one clear, continuous narrative in the words of the authorized King James text. (#Ms116—50¢)

HOW THE GREAT RELIGIONS BEGAN *by Joseph Gaer*

An always timely, easy-to-read guide to man's unending quest for the spiritual, vividly told through the inspiring lives of the world's religious leaders: Jesus, Mohammed, Moses, Buddha, Lao-Tse, and others. (#Ks308—35¢)

GANDHI: His Life and Message for the World
by Louis Fischer

The life story of one of the greatest inspirational and political leaders of our time gives insight into India's pivotal place in world affairs. (#K300—25¢)

OUT OF MY LIFE AND THOUGHT *by Albert Schweitzer*
With Postscript 1932-1949 by Everett Skillings

The remarkable life story of one of the 20th century's greatest men, who renounced a brilliant career as musician, philosopher and theologian to become a medical missionary in Africa. (#MD83—50¢)

TO OUR READERS

We welcome your comments about any SIGNET, SIGNET KEY or MENTOR BOOK, as well as your suggestions for new reprints. If your dealer does not have the books you want, you may order them by mail enclosing the list price plus 5¢ a copy to cover mailing costs. Send for a copy of our complete catalog. The New American Library of World Literature, Inc., 501 Madison Ave., N.Y. 22, N.Y.

THE TEN COMMANDMENTS

by

A. Powell Davies

A SIGNET KEY BOOK
Published by THE NEW AMERICAN LIBRARY

Published as a SIGNET KEY BOOK

FIRST PRINTING, NOVEMBER, 1956
SECOND PRINTING, NOVEMBER, 1956

The author gratefully acknowledges permission to quote from the following works to illustrate the text of this book:

American Schools of Oriental Research: From *What Mean These Stones?* by Millar Burrows, Copyright, 1941, American Schools of Oriental Research.

Harper & Brothers: From *Hebrew Origins* by Theophile J. Meek, Copyright 1936, 1950 by Harper & Brothers, and *Introduction to the Old Testament* by Robert H. Pfeiffer, Copyright 1941, 1948 by Harper & Brothers.

Thomas Nelson & Sons, Ltd. (Edinburgh): From a selection by Gilbert Murray in *Peake's Commentary on the Bible.*

Oxford University Press (London): From an article by R. H. Kennett in "Journal of Theological Studies."

G. P. Putnam's Son (New York) and Williams & Norgate Ltd. (London): From *The Old Testament in the Light of the Ancient East* by Alfred Jeremias.

Fleming H. Revell Company: From *The Archeology of Palestine and the Bible* by William F. Albright, Copyright MCMXXXII, by Fleming H. Revell Co.

Charles Scribner's Sons: From selections in *Encyclopedia of Religion and Ethics,* and article by C. H. W. Johns in *Dictionary of the Bible* (Extra Volume) edited by James Hastings, Copyright, 1904, by Charles Scribner's Sons.

Library of Congress Catalog Card. No. 56-12514

*SIGNET KEY BOOKS are published by
The New American Library of World Literature, Inc.
501 Madison Avenue, New York 22, New York*

PRINTED IN THE UNITED STATES OF AMERICA

CONTENTS

v

THE TEN
COMMANDMENTS

INTRODUCTION

The Scriptures and Modern Scholarship

The story of the Ten Commandments, as preserved by Biblical tradition, is tensely dramatic and has had for many centuries a powerful hold on popular imagination. High on Mt. Sinai, hidden within a dense cloud which is the center of a violent thunderstorm, God hands to Moses two tables of stone, divinely inscribed with the sacred code. While descending the mountain, Moses discovers that the Children of Israel have forsaken the true God who has chosen them to be his people and are worshipping a golden calf. Furious with anger, he breaks the stone tables and grinds the idol into powder.

Later, the people having repented, two substitute tables of stone are provided, which God inscribes as he did the first ones, and these (as the story is usually interpreted) are placed in a specially constructed Ark of the Covenant, which goes with the Children of Israel in their wanderings.

The story told by modern scholars is very different, but, in its own way, equally dramatic. In their case, the drama is not one of supernatural events but of important—and sometimes sensational—discovery. It is because of their work—honest, patient and rigorously disciplined—that we have genuine knowledge of the Scriptures instead of ignorant surmises and interpretations based on superstition. For we must recognize that the Bible, irrespective of the religious viewpoint with which we approach it, presents us with some difficult problems. The more carefully we study it the greater these problems become. There are inconsistencies, contradictions, tantalizing historical questions, riddles of language and text. There are dilemmas posed by archaeological discoveries. There are many obscurities of meaning and uncertainties of time and place.

In the case of the Ten Commandments several of these difficulties become apparent when we notice that two versions are given us, one in Exodus xx (which is the one custom has adopted) and another in Deuteronomy v. Although closely similar for the most part, there are significant differences, the most conspicuous of which is in the Fourth Commandment where we are given widely divergent reasons for observing the Sabbath Day. If, then, the Commandments were inscribed by God on tables of stone, which of the two versions did he inscribe? If, on the other hand, it was Moses who wrote the Ten Commandments, which version did he write?

Even the most traditionalist reader must admit that these are questions which the Bible on the surface does not answer; and to get beneath the surface requires the methods of the scholar.

In reality, however, the problems presented by the Ten Commandments are much wider than the existence of two versions and lead us into a broad field of inquiry in which we shall encounter many puzzling questions. These questions, though often difficult, present us with a fascinating challenge—a challenge which, if we can prove equal to it, not only spurs us to acquire some genuine knowledge of the Bible, but enables us to see the real nature of the immense and long-continued struggle through which man has grown in spiritual stature and raised the level of his religion.

It is a pity that this kind of research is still so often misunderstood and therefore viewed with suspicion. The fear is, apparently—to put it bluntly—that the Bible will not stand investigation. In other areas truth may be sought at all costs, but in the case of the Scriptures there is too much danger that something precious will be lost.

What this implies is that religion is only safe if it is based upon ignorance rather than knowledge, and that the truth which religion exhorts us to serve is nevertheless unfriendly to religion. This position has only to be stated to be seen to be absurd. Truth is indeed an enemy of unfounded beliefs but never of an honest faith. Religion gains, not loses, when its ground becomes that of evidence instead of supposition, of reason and knowledge instead of improbable tradition. What happens as a result of scholarly research is that we come to know how religion *really* developed, how it gradually and painfully made its way from one level to another, how in the mind of man there was a natural evolution of ideas, how in human society there was a slow sloughing off of barbarous customs and an ascent towards benevolence and righteousness.

In depriving us of the shelter of ancient assumptions this is admittedly a more difficult approach at first, and makes us feel that we have lost something. People had the same feeling when they were told by Darwin that man has emerged from the lower animals. Expanding the family album to this extreme extent was something of a strain, and for a time people resisted it. But today we are thoroughly accustomed to this idea and understand the world and ourselves much better because we have accepted the correctness of biological evolution.

We are doing the same—but are not as far advanced— with cultural anthropology. We are adjusting ourselves to new approaches in the social sciences as a whole. We should make similar adjustments in our attitude towards religion. Its basis will thus become much firmer and there will be nothing to fear from the growth of knowledge. In revising our view of religious history and arriving at a more realistic understanding of our sacred Scriptures, we shall lose only what it is better that we lose and shall have a clearer understanding of essentials.

Here we should recognize that in the modern world the Ten Commandments are less important in what they literally convey than as a great religious symbol. If we discover that at the time they were composed the religious level was much lower than it has since become, we are not debasing the value of the Commandments as a sacred symbol. Our debt to the religion of Israel is a great one. It was not through anything miraculous but because of a long and agonizing spiritual pilgrimage that Jewish ethics achieved so high a level and Jewish faith its purity and nobility. The Ten Commandments were a landmark in this pilgrimage. Carried onward, they have become a symbol —sacred not to Jews alone but also in a high degree to

Christians, too—a symbol of a moral law which is still advancing and of a quest for righteousness that is unending.

Unless we have but little faith in truth there is nothing that we need fear from modern scholarship. No study can suffer from examining argument with an open mind or from treating evidence honestly. As to the study that we are ourselves now undertaking we shall press no conclusions upon the reader. He himself shall be the judge; the arguments and the evidence will be laid before him.

CHRONOLOGICAL OUTLINE. I
To The Division Into Two Kingdoms

B.C.

3000-2000 Early Bronze Age. Historical period begins. First dynasty in Egypt, 3000-2700. First Semitic Empire, 2400. Sargon I.

2000-1500 Middle Bronze Age. Mesopotamian and Egyptian Empires. Great migrations throughout Fertile Crescent.

c. 1750 Abraham in Palestine (?)

c. 1700 CODE OF HAMMURABI of Babylon, from which Canaanite law and "Law of Moses" partly derived.

1700-1550 The Hyksos from Canaan control Egypt, permitting settlement (?) of Hebrews on Nile Delta (Goshen); Hebrews begin to settle in Canaan (Palestine).

c. 1550 Hyksos expelled from Egypt. Hittites destroy Babylon.

1500-1200 Late Bronze Age. Period of Egypt's greatest dominance. Canaan an Egyptian province. Letters to Pharaoh tell of Hebrew attacks on Canaanite cities (Amarna tablets).

c. 1400 Jericho destroyed by "Joshua," who had formed Israelite confederation in northern Canaan. Capital: Shechem.

1377-1360 Reign of Pharoah IKHNATON (Amenophis IV), first monotheist in history. His reforms swept away after his death.

c. 1230 Exodus of Israelites (Levites?) from Egypt under MOSES.
TRADITIONAL DATE FOR TEN
COMMANDMENTS

c. 1200 Iron Age begins. Occupation of lands east of the Jordan and of parts of southern Canaan by desert tribes led by Israelites who had escaped from Egypt.

1225-1020 Israelites subdue more of Canaan. Struggle with the Philistines. Rule by sheiks or "judges." Israelite and Canaanite life mingling; Canaanite civilization absorbed.

c. 1020 Israelite tribes partly combine under first king, Saul.

c. 1004 DAVID becomes king of southern Israel, called JUDAH.

998 David becomes king of all Israel. Captures Jerusalem, which becomes capital. Extends Israelite territory to greatest size it ever reached, while international situation unusually favorable.

13

965-926 SOLOMON ruler of united kingdom. Builds first temple at Jerusalem. Reigns in great magnificence. Prosperous trade. But heavy taxation causes resentment and near-mutiny.

c. 926 Kingdom divided: ISRAEL in north; JUDAH in south.

CHRONOLOGICAL OUTLINE. II

From The Two Kingdoms To The Roman Empire

Northern Kingdom:	Southern Kingdom:
B.C.	B.C.
926-907 Jeroboam I	926-910 Rehoboam
871-852 Ahab ⎫ Reforms of 852-851 Ahaziah ⎬ the prophet, ⎭ Elijah	725-697 Hezekiah Prophets Isaiah & Micah
787-747 Jeroboam II Prophet Amos	701 Attempt of Sennacharib to take Jerusalem. Heavy tribute exacted.
746-735 Zechariah to ⎱ Prophet Pekahiah ⎰ Hosea	696-642 Manasseh. Assyrian astral deities worshipped at Jerusalem. Fertility cult. Infant sacrifice. Religious crisis approaching.
721 FALL OF SAMARIA AND END OF THE NORTHERN KINGDOM	

621 Deuteronomic Law promulgated.
FIRST PUBLICATION OF THE TEN COMMANDMENTS (Deuteronomy v version).
Prophets Jeremiah and Ezekiel.
Rise of Babylon.

586 FALL OF JERUSALEM AND BEGINNING OF EXILE in Babylon.

538 Edict of Cyrus, the Persian, permitting return from Exile.
SECOND VERSION OF TEN COMMANDMENTS (Exodus xx) compiled during this period.

520-516 Temple rebuilt by Zerubbabel.

458-444 Ezra and Nehemiah. Restoration of Judah begun, now to be called Judea.

444 Publication and acceptance of the Law codified during the Exile and attributed to Moses, including both versions of the TEN COMMANDMENTS.

333 Alexander the Great enters Jerusalem.

320 Palestine under the Ptolemies (Egypt).

198 Palestine under the Seleucids (Syria).

168 Antiochus IV (Epiphanes) attempts to suppress the Jewish religion.

167-135 Revolt of the Maccabees.

142 Jewish independence of Syria; rule by priest-kings.

65 Pompey enters Jerusalem and Palestine becomes Roman province.

TRADITIONAL JOURNEY
of the
CHILDREN of ISRAEL
in the WILDERNESS

MEDITERRANEAN SEA

Jericho
MT. NEBO
CANAAN
Gaza
DEAD SEA
Beer-Sheba
MOAB
WILDERNESS OF ZIN
EDON
Kadesh
ARABIAN DESERT
Ezion-Geber

SINAI PENINSULA

WILDERNESS OF SIN
Rephidim
MT. SINAI

LAND OF GOSHEN

EGYPT

GULF OF SUEZ

GULF OF AQABAH

LAND OF MIDIAN

RED SEA

CHAPTER ONE

The Traditional Story

1. The Books of Moses

It was long believed that the first five books of the Bible were written by Moses. Even the account of his death and burial, according to the stricter view, came from his pen. But in the books themselves nothing is said about their authorship as a whole: only a few passages are attributed to Moses. It is not until we reach the book of Chronicles, written almost a thousand years later than the time of Moses, that the Bible connects his name with the writing of the first five books.

In Hebrew tradition, the five are counted as one book and are called "the Law of Moses" and sometimes "the five-fifths of the Law." It was only practical convenience that dictated the division into five scrolls. When parchment became available to replace the papyrus that had first been used (papyrus is made from the pith of reeds and was the ancient equivalent of paper), its greater strength permitted the transcription of the entire book on to one long scroll.

There is no doubt that these five books (Genesis, Exodus, Leviticus, Numbers, Deuteronomy) form one work; in fact, the sixth book (Joshua) is also a part of the same continuous narrative, although this was not acknowledged since no claim could be made that Joshua was written by Moses.

In about the second century B.C., the Hebrew Scriptures were translated into Greek, probably in Egypt. This famous translation is called the Septuagint because, traditionally, it was made by seventy (or seventy-two) Jewish elders and was completed in seventy (or seventy-two)

17

days. From the Septuagint is derived the term used to indicate the first five books: the *Pentateuch,* which is merely Greek for "five books."

When Joshua is included, we speak of the *Hexateuch* (*six* books), but in this chapter we shall follow the more traditional arrangement, not examining for the moment the question of authorship. What then does the Bible tell us in the books attributed to Moses?

2. *The Promise and the Covenant*

The Pentateuch opens with two stories of the creation of the world, each in its differing way arresting and beautiful, followed by an additional brief account of the creation of man.[1] In the second of the three stories, in which God frequently visits the first human couple, having a form like their own and talking to them in a "human" voice, we are told of a tree the fruit of which must not be eaten. But Adam and Eve, the newly-created couple, do eat of it, as a result of which they are thrust forth from the Garden of Eden.

Moving rapidly, the narrative then describes the first murder, a fratricide in which Abel, a herdsman, is done to death by his farmer brother, Cain, thus signifying, apparently, the antagonism between the nomadic and agricultural ways of life. After this there is widespread human debauchment, a reign of evil which provokes God to destroy all he had created in a universal, catastrophic flood. One good man, however—the only one that he could find—God decides to save, together with his family. This man, Noah, is instructed to build an enormous ark and to take into it specimen pairs of all the animals (certain verses speak of *seven* pairs in the case of "clean" animals) to replenish the earth when the waters have subsided.

When dry land again appears, Noah and his family are allowed to re-establish human society; and God, sorrowful now at having brought upon the world so vast a measure of calamity, promises that never again will he destroy

[1] I: Gen.i:1—ii:4a; II: Gen.ii: 4b—iv:26; III: Gen.v: 1—2.

by flood the creatures he has made. "While the earth remaineth," he says, "seedtime and harvest, and cold and heat, and summer and winter, and day and night shall not cease." As a pledge of his promise, God puts his rainbow in the sky.

From the sons of Noah the story now traces the derivation of the several human races, and within each race the relationship of tribes and nations. Finally, after an incident in which God becomes alarmed at the universal harmony which is drawing mankind together—which harmony he destroys by "confounding the language of all the earth," so that its peoples become widely scattered—we are given the genealogy that leads us to the central interest of the narrative, the advent of Abraham, descended from Shem.

It is with Abraham that God first initiates his Covenant, promising that he shall be the father of God's chosen people. Moving now at a more leisurely pace, the story introduces the great saga of the patriarchs. Formerly, it was believed that the patriarchs were mythical figures, but it is now known that during the period the Bible describes as that of Abraham, Semitic invaders from the Arabian desert flooded the entire fertile crescent of Mesopotamia from the Persian Gulf up the Tigris and Euphrates valleys to the south of Asia Minor and west to the Mediterranean. There is thus no difficulty in supposing that Abraham was a powerful and wealthy sheik who did migrate from Ur in southern Babylonia to Haran in the north and thence to Palestine.

The promise made to Abraham is renewed to his son, Isaac, and once again a generation later to Jacob, whose name is changed to Israel. But it is a promise frequently deferred. Only after they have endured several centuries of enslavement in Egypt are the descendants of Israel called to be "the people of the Covenant."

3. Egypt and the Exodus

Through Joseph, the favorite son of his father, Israel, the entire family of the aging patriarch is invited to settle in Egypt. Joseph, who has risen to power after an early series of misadventures, beginning with his being sold by his brothers to some passing Bedouins, has been charged by Pharaoh with organizing the storage of surplus grain during good years to provide against years of famine. It is during such a year of famine that he brings his family from Canaan to the delta of the Nile.

With the advent of a new dynasty of pharaohs who cared nothing for the memory of Joseph, the descendants of Israel, now grown numerous, are enslaved. Their condition grows steadily worse until, under one of the pharaohs (probably Rameses II, who used large companies of slaves in his immense construction projects) they are oppressed almost beyond bearing. It is at this point that Moses enters the story.

Desiring to reduce the numbers of the Israelites, Pharaoh orders that all their male children shall be slain at birth, but the midwives who received this order (surprisingly, there are only two of them) refuse to comply. Pharaoh therefore appeals to his Egyptian subjects to carry out the order. Moses' mother, determined to save her baby, places him in a basket which she hides among the reeds in the Nile. Pharaoh's daughter discovers him there and decides to adopt him, which results in Moses receiving all the benefits of noble station and the advantages of an Egyptian education.

But Moses is firm in his allegiance to his own people. In defending one of them from assault he kills an Egyptian and has to flee for his life. This brings him to Midian, across the desert near the Gulf of Akaba, where he finds employment with the priest, Jethro, whose daughter, Zipporah, he takes to wife.

In Midian, attracted by the sight of a flaming bush which burns without being consumed, he walks towards it until he hears a voice which commands him to come no nearer and to take off his shoes since he is standing on holy ground. The voice tells him that the one who is speaking to him is God. The time has come, God says, to deliver the Children of Israel from their Egyptian bondage and to take them into Canaan, "a land flowing with milk and honey," which God will give them to possess. Their emancipator is to be none other than Moses himself, who, after the liberation, will remain their leader and their mediator between themselves and God.

Moses does not want to undertake this mission and pleads his unsuitability, but God insists, promising to sustain him and giving him power to work miracles with a magic rod. When Moses asks by what name God is to be identified to the Children of Israel, he tells him "Jehovah."[2] When Moses points out that he is not a good speaker, God says that Aaron, his brother, will be his spokesman.

Finally, Moses sets out for Egypt, but at a lodging-place on the way a startling incident occurs. Jehovah savagely attacks him and tries to kill him because he is not circumcised. Hastily, his wife, Zipporah, takes a flint knife and circumcises their son, Gershom, touching Moses with the severed foreskin and thereby (as the story seems to indicate but does not actually say) appeases the wrath of Jehovah. This discordant incident will be examined later on; for the moment we notice it only as a strangely jarring episode in the traditional story (Exod. iv: 25-26).

The elders of Israel prepare the people for departure, convinced by the miracles of Moses and the arguments of Aaron that Jehovah is ready to deliver them from bondage. But Pharaoh is reluctant to lose their services and refuses to allow them to leave. Repeatedly, the story tells us, after Moses has inflicted a plague upon Egypt and Pharaoh's attitude has weakened, Jehovah "hardens Pharaoh's heart." After the last plague, however, the "slaying of the first-born," Pharaoh is in haste to have them go.

It is upon this plague—the slaying of the first-born of the Egyptians while the first-born of the Israelites were saved—that the Feast of the Passover is traditionally founded, and the Pentateuch story describes very fully the circumstances in which it was said to be established.

Having "borrowed" from the terrified Egyptians some of their gold and silver and jewels, the Children of Israel set forth, ostensibly on a three-day journey into the wilderness to observe a special festival of Jehovah. Pharaoh,

[2] This conventional name is not correct, as will be explained in due course, but it is the suitable one to use in telling the traditional story. It should be noted that in English translations of the Bible the Hebrew word here given as "Jehovah" is signified by "LORD."

however, who suspects that their departure is intended to be permanent, sends an army to recapture them. By a miracle, the waters of the Red Sea[3] are divided and the Israelites pass over on "dry ground." The Egyptian army, its chariot wheels mired in the mud, makes but poor progress and when the waters return the entire army is drowned.

By slow stages, the Children of Israel make their way southward to the Wilderness of Sin.[4] Several times they are short of water, then of food. Both are miraculously provided. Moving from the Wilderness of Sin east to Rephidim, they encounter the Amalekites with whom they fight a severe battle, which eventually they win. Jethro, his father-in-law, brings to Moses his wife and two sons and suggests a plan for organizing the community under "rulers of thousands, rulers of hundreds, rulers of fifties and rulers of tens." This plan is adopted and soon thereafter the Children of Israel are led south to the Wilderness of Sinai where they "camped before the mount."

4. Sinai, the Mount of Jehovah

In the Pentateuch the events of Mount Sinai are unquestionably the focal point of history. Here, Jehovah makes his covenant with his people. Here, Moses, the greatest man of all time, goes up to talk with Jehovah as a man talks with his friend. Sinai seems to be, in a peculiar way, Jehovah's dwelling-place. It is sacred and thus dangerous, and the people are warned not to come close to the mountain "lest Jehovah break forth upon them."

Even in the traditional story, read just as it is written, Jehovah seems to be a somewhat localized God, "going down" to see for himself what is happening at Babel or at Sodom and Gomorrah. From time to time (assuming for the moment his identity with the God who appears to the patriarchs) he is found in Canaan; he accompanies the Israelites in their exodus from Egypt. Now, however, he

[3] The Hebrew יַם־סוּף should be translated *sea* or *lake of reeds* rather than *Red Sea*.
[4] Pronounced *seen* and meaning "Moon" or "Moon-God."

seems to be in his own habitation, and it is here that he makes his covenant that Israel shall be his chosen people.

The Children of Israel are to be "a peculiar treasure" to him, "a kingdom of priests and a holy nation." It is for this purpose that he has borne them "on eagles' wings" out of Egypt. He asks Moses to make inquiry of the people whether they are willing to enter into this covenant. Moses calls the elders and conveys the message and the people are assembled together to give their answer. They solemnly pledge themselves to be governed by the terms of the covenant. "All that Jehovah hath spoken, we will do."

Moses reports this answer to Jehovah, who thereupon announces that he will come to him "in a thick cloud" and the people will hear his voice, after which they should be willing to believe Moses "forever." After ceremonies of sanctification lasting two days, during which clothing is ritually washed and sexual intercourse forbidden, on the morning of the third day Moses brings the people to the foot of the mountain.

Then began "thunders and lightnings, and a thick cloud on the mount, and the voice of a trumpet exceeding loud: and all the people that were in the camp trembled." Still louder blared the trumpet, and upon this signal Moses spoke to Jehovah and "God answered him by a voice." Then Moses was told to leave the people and come up to the top of the mountain where God was waiting for him.

It was at this time, *according to tradition*, that God handed to Moses the two stone tables upon which he had inscribed the Ten Commandments—*but not according to the Bible*. At this point we are in trouble, no matter how much we want to follow the Biblical narrative literally. Nevertheless, let us *try* to follow it literally.

5. *The Stone Tables of Testimony*

In Exodus xix we are told that Moses had no sooner ascended the mountain than Jehovah told him to go down again and warn the people not to try to "break through unto the Lord and gaze, and many of them perish." Moses reminds Jehovah that there is little likelihood of this since the people have already been warned that death is the penalty if they fail to observe the boundaries. Whereupon Jehovah instructs Moses to go down in any case and bring up Aaron, but not the priests or the people. The chapter ends with the words, "So Moses went down unto the people and told them."

Then, without any indication that Moses has returned to the mountain, the twentieth chapter begins: "And God spake all these words, saying, I am Jehovah, thy God, which brought thee out of the land of Egypt, out of the house of bondage. Thou shalt have no other gods before me"—and the passage continues with the other nine of the Ten Commandments. When the Commandments are concluded, we are told that the people trembled at the thunderings and the lightnings and begged that Moses, not God, be the one who speaks to them, for of God they are mortally afraid. After reassuring them that God is only testing them, Moses draws near "unto the thick darkness" where God is, and God tells him to remind the Children of Israel of what they have seen, and then—with interruptions—continues with further laws and ordinances for eleven chapters.

Twice during these eleven chapters, Moses reascends the mountain, once with Aaron, Nadab, Abihu, and seventy of the elders of Israel, and once with Joshua, although it is not clear how many times he has come down. During one of the intervals that he spends with the people, he writes down "all the words of the Lord," builds an altar and offers an elaborate sacrifice, and reads aloud the entire Book of the Covenant. It is after this solemn occasion that he takes Aaron, Nadab, Abihu, and seventy of the elders of Israel with him up the mountain, where they actually see the God of Israel and eat and drink in his presence. Then follows the ascent with Joshua, Jehovah having at last promised that he will give to Moses "the tables of stone, and the law and the commandment," but there is no mention of what is inscribed on the tables of stone and no indication that at this time Jehovah fulfils his promise.

Then, astonishingly, in the thirty-second chapter of

Exodus, we are told of contact being renewed with the waiting Israelites, *just as though Moses had not several times returned and visited with them*. The people, in fact, have waited so long in vain that they have become weary of their vigil and have persuaded Aaron to make them an idol, a golden calf, to represent Jehovah. That it is Jehovah that is represented there seems to be no doubt, since the celebration, in the words of Aaron, "shall be a feast to Jehovah." God informs Moses of the "apostasy"[5] that is taking place at the foot of the mountain and announces that he will "consume" the Israelites and make of Moses "a great nation." With patient tactfulness, Moses dissuades Jehovah from this course of action, appealing to his better judgment until at last he repents "of the evil which he said he would do unto his people."

Moses is now free to come down from the mountain, and this time he carries with him the two tables of stone; "tables," the passage tells us, "that were written on both their sides." But we are not told what it was that was written, only that they were the "two tables of the testimony," and that "the tables were the work of God, and the writing was the writing of God."

These were the stone tables that, in his anger, Moses shattered when he saw the "apostasy" of the people. To atone for this "apostasy," he orders a massacre, and we are told that at his instigation the Levites slew "three thousand men." In addition to this, Jehovah himself also "smote the people, because they made the calf, which Aaron made."

By this time a sacred tent has been provided, to which Jehovah comes in a "pillar of cloud," and it is here that he now talks with Moses. But not invariably. For Moses is instructed to hew two tables of stone "like unto the first" and bring them to the top of Mount Sinai, this time alone. Moses does so and Jehovah gives him—orally— another and *different* set of "Commandments"[6] at the end of which Moses is instructed to write them down, the

[5]It is not really an apostasy if it is still Jehovah who is being worshipped, though both he and Moses, according to the text, assume that it is. For the purpose of proceeding with the narrative, we also will assume it.
[6] Given on p. 75-76 (Exed. xxxiv) (Their number could be counted either as ten or twelve)

obvious reference being to the new set of commandments which Jehovah has just uttered. So that when we read the concluding words of the passage, in which we are told that Moses "wrote upon the tables the words of the covenant, the ten commandments," we are utterly confused as to which set of ten commandments it was that were finally written down.

We can abate this confusion somewhat by leaving Exodus and going to Deuteronomy—provided we completely forget the story in Exodus. In Deuteronomy v, where the Ten Commandments are again given, though in a somewhat different version (especially as to the Fourth Commandment), we are told that Jehovah "wrote them upon two tables of stone" and that "he added no more." This last statement contradicts, of course, the account in Exodus, where "he added" a great deal more, and even seems to cast reproach upon it.

For the present, however, we shall not pursue this contradiction further, since by now it is self-evident that from a plain reading of the Bible itself it is impossible to discover what was on the tables of stone.

6. The Mystery of the Death of Moses

In addition to the Ten Commandments the Pentateuch gives us a considerable amount of other legislation—moral, civil, and liturgical—but it plays only a small part in the traditional story. We shall therefore complete our summary by recalling that after the Sinai period there was considerable "wandering in the wilderness," followed at last by the invasion of land east of the Jordan where successful battles acquired for the tribes of Israel the territory that gave them a base from which to attack Canaan itself.

Because of an unspecified sin that he had committed, Moses was not allowed to go with the Israelites into the land to which he had led them. Knowing that his death was near, he therefore called the people to him and reviewed their pilgrimage, their codes of law, and their covenant with Jehovah. After his final exhortation, he gave them his blessing and ascended Mount Nebo where God showed him the "land flowing with milk and honey" which he himself would never enter; and then, as the Pentateuch puts it, "Moses the servant of Jehovah died there in the land of Moab . . . but no man knoweth of his sepulchre unto this day."

Thus, to the mystery of what was on the tables of stone we must add the mystery of Moses' death and burial. What sin was it that was so serious that Moses was not allowed to enter the Promised Land? And why was he secretly buried so that "no man knoweth of his sepulchre"?

At the time of his death Moses was in perfect health. "His eye was not dim," says this final passage of the Pentateuch, "nor his natural force abated" (Deut. xxxiv: 7). But Jehovah's will was that he die in Moab; he must not cross the Jordan into Canaan. Why?

The traditional story does not tell us.

And so we leave it and take up the story told by scholars.

THE SOURCES OF THE PENTATEUCH
or First Five Books of the Bible

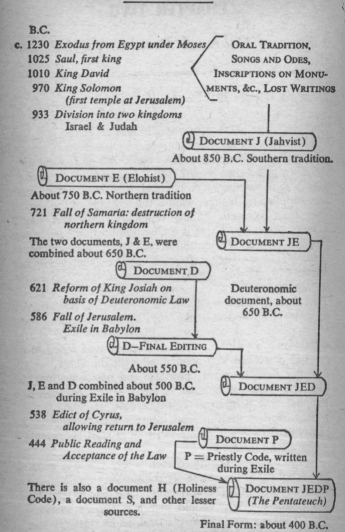

B.C.

c. 1230 *Exodus from Egypt under Moses*

1025 *Saul, first king*

1010 *King David*

970 *King Solomon
(first temple at Jerusalem)*

933 *Division into two kingdoms*
Israel & Judah

ORAL TRADITION,
SONGS AND ODES,
INSCRIPTIONS ON MONU-
MENTS, &C., LOST WRITINGS

DOCUMENT J (Jahvist)

About 850 B.C. Southern tradition.

DOCUMENT E (Elohist)

About 750 B.C. Northern tradition

721 *Fall of Samaria: destruction of
northern kingdom*

The two documents, J & E, were
combined about 650 B.C.

DOCUMENT JE

DOCUMENT D

621 *Reform of King Josiah on
basis of Deuteronomic Law*

586 *Fall of Jerusalem.
Exile in Babylon*

Deuteronomic
document, about
650 B.C.

D—FINAL EDITING

About 550 B.C.

J, E and D combined about 500 B.C.
during Exile in Babylon

DOCUMENT JED

538 *Edict of Cyrus,
allowing return to Jerusalem*

444 *Public Reading and
Acceptance of the Law*

DOCUMENT P

P = Priestly Code, written
during Exile

There is also a document H (Holiness
Code), a document S, and other lesser
sources.

DOCUMENT JEDP
(*The Pentateuch*)

Final Form: about 400 B.C.

There are two versions of the Ten Commandments, one in Document
D, the other in Document P.

CHAPTER TWO

Fact and Fable: A Problem for Scholars

---

1. Who Wrote the Books of Moses?

The tradition that Moses was the author of the first five books of the Bible, although tenaciously held, has always been difficult to maintain. How could Moses have written the story of his own death? And if, as some of the ancient rabbis conceded might be possible, this particular passage was supplied by Joshua, what is the meaning of the words, "No man knoweth of his sepulchre unto this day"? (Deut. xxxiv: 6). There is a clear implication here of the passage of time: *unto this day.* Surely whoever wrote these words lived long after the death of Moses. Neither Moses himself, nor Joshua, could conceivably have written them.

Moreover, when we read that "there hath not arisen a prophet since in Israel like unto Moses," not only must we suppose that considerable time has elapsed during which such a prophet could have arisen and failed to do so, but if we are well acquainted with the Bible, we remember that the word "prophet" did not come into use until the time of Samuel. ("He that is now called a Prophet was beforetime called a Seer" I Sam. ix: 9). Moses lived in the thirteenth century B.C., Samuel in the eleventh. So the authorship must be at least two hundred years after Moses.

It did not pass unnoticed even before the time of modern scholarship that there were disturbing implications in such sayings as "The Canaanite was then in the land" (Gen. xii: 6). Why should such a statement be made if the Canaanite was *still* in the land, as he certainly was at the time of Moses? To draw a comparison, we might ask why an American would say, "There were Indians then on Manhattan Island," if he were living at a time when

Indians still possessed it. He would only speak in such terms after—and probably considerably after—the Indians had left.

Again, in Genesis (xxxvi: 31) we read, "These are the kings that reigned in the land of Edom before there reigned any king over the children of Israel." Could this be written *before* there were kings in Israel? For Moses to have been the author of such a statement is as though one of the Pilgrim Fathers had said, "These are the kings that reigned in France before there was any president of the United States." The Pilgrim Fathers had no way of knowing that there ever would be a president of the United States. In the same way there was nothing that Moses could foresee about kings in Israel.

Since the first king of Israel was Saul, who reigned during the last quarter of the eleventh century B.C., this is the earliest date that this passage could have been composed. By this time Moses had been dead for the greater part of two centuries.

A further passage (Gen. xiv: 14) tells us that Abraham pursued his enemies as far as the city of Dan. But we know from the book of Judges (xviii: 29) that this city, the earlier name of which was Laish, did not receive the name Dan until considerably after the time of Moses. Was there any way by which Moses could have foreseen that Laish was going to be called Dan?

Considerations of which these are examples led early scholars to question the tradition that Moses wrote the Pentateuch. Ibn Ezra, in the twelfth century A.D., gave cryptic indications of his doubts but prudently refrained from open statements of them. Spinoza, in the seventeenth century, not only rejected the Mosaic authorship but developed some of the beginnings of the methods of modern scholarship. More outspoken than Ibn Ezra, he was excommunicated from the synagogue.

It is impossible to trace in any detail here the history of Biblical criticism[1] as it applies to the Pentateuch.

---

[1] The word *criticism* as used by scholars does not imply anything destructive; it derives from the Greek, κριτικός (criticos) and means (literally) skilled judgment. Scholarly criticism is scientific investigation leading to informed opinion and authoritative evaluation.

Suffice it to say that not only was Mosaic authorship disproved but it was discovered that the Pentateuch (actually the Hexateuch, since the book of Joshua is a part of the same work) was not written by any one person or even during any one lifetime but is composed of several sources which are plainly traceable and which come from periods as widely separated as the ninth century and the fourth century B.C. A few fragments, chiefly songs, are somewhat older.[2]

We shall now pay some attention to these sources seeking to discover what light they throw on the general character of the Pentateuch, as part of our equipment for understanding the special problem of the Ten Commandments.

2. *The Sources of the Pentateuch*

The key to the sources of the Pentateuch might be found in many places; we shall choose, as did Astruc, the early scholar, the sixth chapter of the book of Exodus. Here (vi: 2-3) God says to Moses, "I am Yahweh[3]: and I appeared unto Abraham, unto Isaac, and unto Jacob as El Shaddai, but by my name Yahweh I was not known to them." What this means is that Yahweh is introducing

[2] The bibliography on p. 136 indicates resources to which the reader may turn for a fuller treatment of the results of modern Biblical scholarship.

[3] This is the correct name, not *Jehovah*, the name we temporarily used while telling the traditional story. The word *Yahweh* (Hebrew: יהוה) was considered (and still is) too sacred to be spoken aloud and therefore the word *Adonai*, meaning Lord, was substituted. Where *Adonai* was used as a preceding word (the Lord Yahweh), *Elohim*, meaning God (formerly plural, *gods*), was used. There were no vowels in ancient Hebrew, and when, later, they were supplied (as "points" written mostly beneath the line), those for *Adonai* or *Elohim* were used in the case of the sacred name *Yahweh*, to indicate the pronunciation of *the word to be spoken*, not the word written. (יְהֹוָה) Jews understood this, but Christians did not. The latter, therefore, supplied the *Adonai* vowels to YHWH, making YaHoWaH, or *Jehovah*. The word in this conflate form has long been in general use and under ordinary circumstances it is just as well to use it. But in a discussion such as we are embarked upon, it is necessary to indicate quite precisely the "Sinai-Midian" God who was one of many gods but who, in the evolution of Hebrew religion, gradually became the one and only God. We must therefore use the word "Yahweh." In English Bibles, the word *Elohim* is translated "God," *Yahweh* is given as "the LORD" (capital letters), and *Adonai* is translated "the Lord" (*not* capitals).

himself by that name *for the first time*. To the patriarchs he had been El Shaddai, their family God from Haran, from which Abraham had come;[4] or simply God (Elohim).

But contrary to the implications of this passage we find the name Yahweh quite freely used in the Pentateuch, almost from the beginning. We find that God does identify himself by that name to the patriarchs. To Abraham he says, "I am Yahweh that brought thee out of Ur of the Chaldees" (Gen. xv: 7). To Jacob he says, "I am Yahweh, the God of Abraham, thy father, and the God of Isaac" (Gen. xxviii: 13). Even as early as the fourth chapter of Genesis, we find it stated that "then men began to call upon the name of Yahweh."

On the basis of the Pentateuch coming from a single author (or even a group of authors, writing in collaboration), these divergences are incomprehensible. One part of the narrative flatly contradicts another and in so flagrant a way that no single author or cooperating group of authors could possibly have overlooked it.

We have taken a single example. But there are many others. If the reader will turn to the book of Genesis he will discover that chapter one and chapter two down to the word "created" in the fourth verse give a complete summary of the work of creation. With the second half of this verse, however (Gen. ii: 4b), a new story, begins and a quite different one. In the first story for instance, God (Elohim) creates man, male and female, on the sixth day. It is the culminating act of creation. But in the second story a single man (no female) is formed by God (Yahweh-Elohim) out of the dust of the earth before there is any vegetation, and God plants a garden for him. Only then does God (Yahweh-Elohim) create the animals, hoping that a species will emerge that will be a fit companion (mate?) for the man. None is satisfactory, so he makes a woman out of one of the man's ribs while he sleeps.

Now, if it is noticed that in the first story the name for

---

[4] *El Shaddai* was formerly mistranslated "God Almighty," and this mistranslation appears in all our Bibles. See article in *Westminster Historical Atlas to the Bible*, Philadelphia, 1945, p. 26; also archeological reports; see bibliography.

God is Elohim while in the second it is Yahweh-Elohim, and if it is observed that as we proceed through the Pentateuch this alternation of passages with first the one name for God and then the other constantly recurs, it gives us a suggestion. Suppose the Elohim passages come from one source, formerly a separate document, and the Yahweh-Elohim passages from another? Suppose these sources in many respects differ in the account they give of the same events? Suppose they have been combined without being harmonized?

Taking this suggestion and applying it to the entire Pentateuch, scholars have long since discovered that it explains completely the many discrepancies. In the one source a single pair of each species of animal is taken by Noah into the ark; in the other source seven pairs are taken of the "clean" animals. In the one source Joseph is sold by his brothers to Midianites; in the other to Ishmaelites. Here, too, we find the explanation of our difficulties with the story of Moses and Mount Sinai. What we were dealing with was a composite narrative, composed of fragments fitted together but not harmonized. What happened according to one source was different from what happened according to another. But the editor, who felt free to combine the fragments, did not feel free to re-write them—or at least not extensively. And so it is throughout the Pentateuch.

Except that this over-simplifies the matter. There are not two sources but four main ones and a number of lesser ones. The four main ones are known as J (Jahvist)[5], E (Elohist), D (Deuteronomic), P (Priestly). They are separated from one another not merely on the basis of the name used for God, but also on that of language, style, and all the indications of internal evidence. We can now see very easily how the passage in Exodus vi can be

[5]Jahveh is merely the German spelling of Yahweh. The pronunciation is the same. The early pre-eminence of German scholars in Biblical criticism led to the wide adoption of their symbols. Hence J for Yahwist instead of Y.

AN EXAMPLE OF THE SEPARATION OF A BIBLE PASSAGE INTO ITS DOCUMENTARY SOURCES

P   *6. And Noah was six hundred years old when the flood of waters was upon the earth.* 7. And Noah went in, and his sons, and his wife, and his son's wives with him, into the

J   ark, because of the waters of the flood. 8. Of clean beasts, and of beasts that are not clean, and of fowls, and of everything that creepeth upon the ground, 9. there went in *two and two*† unto Noah into the ark, *male and female,*† as *God**† commanded Noah. 10. And it came to pass after the seven days, that the waters of the flood were upon the earth. 11.

P   *In the six hundredth year of Noah's life, in the second month, on the seventeenth day of the month, on the same day were all the fountains of the great deep broken up, and the windows of heaven were opened. 12. And the* rain was upon the earth forty days and

J   forty nights. 13. *In the self-same day entered Noah, and Shem, and Ham, and Japheth, the sons of Noah, and Noah's wife, and the three wives of his sons with them, into the ark;*

P   *14. they, and every beast after its kind, and all the cattle after their kind, and every creeping thing that creepeth upon the earth after its kind, and every fowl after its kind, every bird of every sort. 15. And they went in unto Noah into the ark, two and two of all flesh wherein is the breath of life. 16. And they that went in, went in male and female of all*

P & J   *flesh, as God* commanded him;* and the LORD** shut him in. 17. *And the flood was* forty days *upon the earth;* and the waters increased and bare up the ark, and it was lift

J   up above the earth. 18. *And the waters pre-*

P   *vailed, and increased greatly upon the earth; and the ark went upon the face of the waters.*

P = the Priestly Document, written during the Exile, sixth century, B.C.
J = the Jahvist (Yahwist) Document, the oldest of the main sources, written about 850 B.C. in Judah, the southern kingdom. The two other main sources, E and D, do not appear in this passage.
†Interpolations from P.
**Elohim.*
‡Verses 12 and 16b originally stood after verse 9.
***Yahweh.*

34

explained. In one of the sources God is never called Yahweh until the moment that he appears to Moses and gives this as his name. In another source, the Jahvist, God is called Yahweh from the beginning. What we have are two different stories from two (or more) different writers.

Although we cannot go into the matter here, the reader should know that these sources have in turn been subdivided and that in certain passages of the Pentateuch there is material from outside them. An important additional source is H, the "Holiness Code" of Leviticus xvii to xxvi. The Biblical scholar, Pfeiffer, one of the foremost in the field, finds an S document (which he subdivides) coming not from Israel but from Edom, which explains passages which are pro-Edomite and hostile to Israel.[6] To this document, revising the views of earlier scholars, he also ascribes the creation narrative generally attributed to J.

D, or the Deuteronomic document, is largely the book of Deuteronomy itself, and we can now see why it has a different version of the Ten Commandments from that given in Exodus. It was originally independent of Exodus. We also know, in the case of Deuteronomy, the date of its publication, 621 B.C., when it became the basis of the reforms instituted by King Josiah. We know, too, that it cannot have been written much before this time and that its author, who had a very distinctive and recognizable style, was much influenced by the prophets of the eighth and seventh centuries who first gave emphasis to God's call for righteousness.

Since detailed treatment is beyond our scope we shall now characterize the main sources of the Pentateuch and give their dates. J, the most picturesque and colorful of the sources, derives its material from folklore tradition with some indebtedness, no doubt, to previous writings and from the history and legends connected with shrines. The emphasis is southern—Judah rather than the north-

---

6 See Robert H. Pfeiffer, *Introduction to the Old Testament* (rev. ed.). New York: Harper & Brothers, 1948. The most authoritative treatment available (in English), and embodying recent research. S. R. Driver's books are classics but must be largely supplemented by reports of more recent findings.

ern kingdom. Its date is about 850 B.C. E, which eliminates all appearances of God to mortals, except Moses, idealizes its characters more than J but belongs to the same class of literature. Date: about 750 B.C. J and E were combined by an editor in about 650 B.C.

Of Deuteronomy we have already spoken. The original version, published in 621 B.C., was several times expanded and edited, perhaps for the last time about 550 B.C. It was then combined with JE, producing (with additional material) JED. This was during the Exile in Babylon, after the destruction of Jerusalem in 586 B.C. by Nebuchadnezzar. P, the Priestly Code, was produced entirely during the Exile and it is in this source that we find the Ten Commandments in Exodus xx. About 400 B.C., P was added to JED and the Pentateuch took almost its present form.[7]

3. Myth, Legend and History

That the Pentateuch contains authentic history we need not doubt. Much of it, however, can only be discovered by digging beneath the surface. Most of us, including many traditionalists, have long since conceded that the stories of Creation and of the Great Flood are myths, revised from those of the Babylonians. If we were to take these stories literally we would have to agree with Archbishop Usher that the world was created in 4,004 B.C., and that before that date there was nothing but chaos. But we know positively that by this time the world had been a going concern for quite a long while and that even man, a late arrival, had almost completed a Stone Age of over 200,000 years and was beginning to make tools and weapons out of copper. We are equally sure that,

7 Pfeiffer, *op. cit.* pp. 129-209; also all modern commentaries. See bibliography, p. 137. This rather technical subject is difficult to present to the general reader in an immediately comprehensible form. But anyone who will spend a few moments studying the "pictographic" chart on p. 28, and who, from time to time, will take the trouble to refer back to this chart will gain a good grasp of essentials. It is also strongly recommended that the reader refer, whenever he is uncertain about chronological relationships, to the table provided on p. 13. If a few important dates are well remembered everything related to them becomes much more intelligible.

although there have been great upheavals in the earth, some of which caused massive inundations, there is no possibility that Noah could have survived one, together with specimens of all living species—they would run into millions—which he had collected and placed in an ark. All this we look upon as poetry, delightful to read but unrelated to fact.

Not many of us believe that the patriarchs lived to be several hundred years old; the evidence is entirely that man has had about the same optimum life-span ever since he emerged. Nor are we likely to take too literally the story of Sarah, wife of Abraham, who in the eighteenth chapter of Genesis is described as "stricken in age" and in the twentieth, is so irresistible that King Abimelech of Gerar insists that he must have her in his harem— Abraham (for security reasons) having passed her off as his sister!

Just as we know that what we are dealing with in the Creation and Flood stories is myth, so in the case of Abraham and the patriarchs we know that we are dealing with legend. In the case of legend, however, there is usually a basis in history. Because the story of Abraham as we have it is incredible, it is not necessary to suppose that Abraham himself did not exist.

When we come from the time of the patriarchs to the time of the Exodus, we are nearer to the likelihood of actual history. But knowing the nature of the earlier narrative we should expect that here, too, there will be much that is legendary. What we are dealing with is tradition, at first oral tradition, which gathered into itself all the miracles and marvels that the story could be made to carry. Both those who told the stories and those who heard them wanted them that way: they were not interested in authenticity, they wanted to enchant and be enchanted, to bedazzle and to be amazed. It is in this context that we should evaluate the wonders done by Moses, putting to naught the Egyptian wizards through the superior sorcery of his magic rod. But the enslavement of the Israelites may be historical and so may their departure, under Moses, from the delta of the Nile.

Coming down to the occupation of Palestine we can

anticipate that the historical elements in the narrative will increase, but we must still look for legend. What we read belongs to the same sources as the earlier stories and has not in the least lost their characteristics; one of them has even been magnified: the desire to glorify ancestral exploits and to add lustre to the ancient heroes.

In the period after the occupation, when Israel was "ruled" by chief sheiks or "judges," the historical element may again be expected to increase. But it still needs careful sifting out. It is not until the chronicle is written at a time near to the events it describes that we can feel that in the main what we are reading is what actually occurred. If now, however, there is less of legend there is an increased need to watch out for changes made by editors to align the story with their views.

Some of these same editorial changes—and even quite large insertions—go back into the earlier material, too. All that is told, for instance, about the provisions for sacrificing in the wilderness—or almost all—belongs to a far later time. We know that this is so for many reasons, but one that will be instantly plain to the general reader is the rhetorical question asked by the prophet Amos (eighth century B.C.), who was strongly opposed to sacrifice. "Did ye bring unto me sacrifices and offerings in the wilderness forty years, O House of Israel?" he inquires (Amos v: 25). The implication is quite obvious: his argument is that Israel ought not to offer sacrifice; and his point of reference is a former time of great importance in the national saga, *at which former time there was no sacrificing,* namely, in the wilderness. Most of the material in the Pentateuch, therefore, which provides for the tabernacle and its altars of sacrifice, is fictitious—not legendary, now, but deliberately unhistorical material written for a purpose.

To take another illustration of later customs being attributed to earlier times we have in Deuteronomy xxi a law prescribing the correct procedure when an Israelite man marries a foreign woman whom he has taken captive in war. There is nothing whatever to indicate disapproval of such marriages. But in Deuteronomy vii, an earlier chapter *written and inserted later,* marriage with a foreigner is strictly forbidden on pain of being destroyed by Yahweh.

Such illustrations might be continued indefinitely. But a few are enough to suggest all that we intend to convey in this section, namely, that if we wish to separate the historical from the unhistorical in the Pentateuch—as indeed in most other parts of the Bible—we certainly cannot do it merely by reading what is written. Only by scholarly investigation can we know what is history and what is not. And the findings of scholarly investigation are very different from the assumptions transmitted by tradition.

4. *The Bible and Archeology*

From no other source has the Biblical scholar received so much assistance as from archeology. City after city in western Asia, including many in and about Palestine, has been systematically excavated and from the findings it has often been possible to establish quite conclusively what otherwise would have been regarded as still open to debate.

The priority, for instance, of the Babylonian myth of the Creation to the Bible version could be disputed—and was—when the evidence was merely literary and went no farther back than the fourth century B.C. But the discovery in Nineveh, a century ago, of cuneiform tablets datable to about 2000 B.C., on which this myth is inscribed, entirely ends the controversy.

The more recent discoveries at Ras Shamrah, on the Syrian coast north of ancient Phoenicia, also include mythological texts (about 1600 B.C.) as well as a great deal of material that illustrates the Canaanite religious beliefs and practices which later became those of Israel. The continuity of Canaanite and Israelite culture is shown in these tablets in many ways, including the evidence of their own literary connection with the Old Testament prophets. The vocabulary of Phoenician and Israelite is the same and so are many of the ideas.

From the Ras Shamrah discoveries we know that Psalm 29, in our Bible, is based on a Phoenician hymn. A passage in these tablets is quoted by Isaiah (xiv: 12-15). We see from this discovery that the book of Proverbs imitates a Canaanite model. In case after case archeological findings show us the relationship of Israelite religion and literature to those of Canaan, Babylon, Egypt, and indeed to most of the surrounding countries. One of the most interesting examples is the derivation of Psalm 104 from Pharaoh Ikhnaton's "Hymn to the Sun."

A prominent example of the way in which archeology has confirmed the work of Biblical scholars is the case of Jericho and other cities which were supposed to have been destroyed by Joshua. If Joshua destroyed Jericho he could not have destroyed the other cities because they fell more than a century later. On the other hand, if he destroyed the other cities he could not have destroyed Jericho. Ai, which the Bible story says he destroyed immediately after Jericho, is proved by archeological findings to have perished more than five hundred years earlier! What we see here (to summarize abruptly what could only be fully reported in many pages) is confirmation of the scholars' hypothesis that a great deal of Canaan was occupied by Israelites long before the Exodus, and an increased probability that at this earlier time the leader was a man called Joshua who was connected with Moses only by later tradition.

From the Tell el-'Amarna tablets, discovered at the site of the royal city of Amenhotep IV—the famous pharaoh who inaugurated a monotheist reform and changed his name to Ikhnaton (Akhenaton)—we have further confirmation that there were Hebrews (Habiru) in Canaan in the fourteenth century. These tablets, which were letters from Canaanite princes to the imperial government in Egypt,[8] repeatedly complain of Hebrew depredations and invasions. There is also an Egyptian monument which records a battle in which Pharaoh Merneptah defeated "the people of Israel" in Palestine, in about 1230 B.C. This would seem to indicate that Israelites had been in Canaan for some time before the date that most of the evidence

[8] The Tell el-'Amarna tablets, discovered in 1887 (not by archeologists but by an Egyptian peasant-woman), are in cuneiform script, written in Akkadian (Babylonian) but showing Canaanite influence. It was from Canaanitish that written Hebrew was developed.

assigns to the Exodus, which is this same date—unless Pharaoh intervened in the campaigns of "Joshua," a possibility of which the Bible gives no slightest hint. Indeed, what we now know from archeological exploration is that from about the beginning of the sixteenth century B.C. the population of Canaan began to change. There were Amorites (to which group Abraham had probably belonged), Hittites (from a strong civilization in Asia Minor), Perizzites, Hivites, Jebusites (the latter probably the inhabitants of the almost impregnable city of Jerusalem, finally taken by David at the end of the tenth century) Habiri (undoubtedly meaning Hebrews), and possibly Israelite tribes related to the Habiri but politically distinct from them, as well as the original Canaanites.

These are a few out of many possible illustrations of the way in which archeology is corroborating—and supplementing—the findings of modern scholars in their work on the Bible.[9]

5. Uncovering the Evidence

It will now perhaps be seen how hopeless is the attempt to understand the events recorded in the Bible merely by reading what the Bible says. For devotional purposes the Bible—or many parts of it—may be read, of course, for the inspiration the reader derives from it. Or it may be read as great literature—which it most certainly is. With this, however, our present inquiry is not concerned. Our study is historical. We want to know what really happened in Hebrew history that produced the story of Sinai and the several sets of Ten Commandments and what the Commandments meant when they first were promulgated; and finally we desire to see what place this code should take in the history of the development of religion and morality.

To understand these matters we need to solve the problems of the text and get a grasp of the historical context.

[9] A good summary of archeological findings down to about 1940 may be found in Professor Millar Burrows' *What Mean These Stones?* New Haven: American Schools of Oriental Research, 1941. For more recent findings, it is necessary to turn to the archeological journals.

We need to have some idea of the methods scholars use and of the dependability of the findings at which they have arrived. And, as we have begun to see, it is not one area alone to which the investigator must go but many, if he would uncover the evidence. It is only when material from many sources has been painstakingly drawn together and objectively studied that the data can be presented in a form that becomes meaningful. Then must come analysis, the consideration of relationships, the definition and testing of alternative hypotheses.

Or to put the matter more colloquially, a great deal of work must be done before we "know how to ask the right questions." Before we ask what Moses *did,* for instance, we must ask who he was—and even perhaps *whether* he was. To do this we must see how various possibilities fit into what we know—or, where we do not know, whether we can build up probabilities suggested by the evidence. Each tentative solution must be weighed against other tentative solutions and must take its place within the wider scheme of the total problem to see whether it usefully belongs there. Above all, theory and knowledge must be separated.

We *know,* for instance, without reasonable doubt, that some desert tribesmen known as Hebrews and who called themselves Israelites did over a period of time settle in the land of Canaan. We know the centuries during which the settlement took place. But we do not know—we must patiently theorize—about an enslavement in Egypt and an exodus. In the same way we know without reasonable doubt at what time the Scriptural material in which the Ten Commandments are embedded was composed and edited, but we frequently cannot be certain at what time each chapter and verse took the form at which it finally arrived. What we *can* be certain of is that it was a gradual evolutionary process.

THE KINGDOMS
of
ISRAEL and JUDAH

KINGDOM
OF
DAMASCUS

PHOENICIA

Tyre

MEDITERRANEAN SEA

BASHAN

KINGDOM OF
ISRAEL

Samaria

Shechem

RIVER JORDAN

AMMON

Jericho

Jerusalem

PHILISTINES

KINGDOM
OF
JUDAH

Beer-Sheba

MOAB

ARABIAN
DESERT

EDOM

CHAPTER THREE

Moses *and* Mount Sinai

1. When Was the Exodus?

It is perfectly possible to account for the two Hebrew kingdoms in Canaan—Israel in the north, Judah in the south—even if there was no invasion whatever by Israelites who had escaped from Egypt. Archeological findings have made almost certain what the Scriptures themselves had led scholars to suspect. Hebrew invaders were menacing Canaan a century and a half before Moses is likely to have led any Israelites out of Egypt; and even apart from these latest Hebrew invaders it seems likely that earlier Hebrews had long since been settled at such centers as Shechem and in the hill country on which Abraham traditionally had grazed his flocks and herds.

It is easier, however, to account for the two kingdoms if we suppose that, for the most part, the northern area was gradually dominated by Israelites who had never been in Egypt, whereas the southern area was subdued by Israelites who had. This is not to say that all the Israelites who came to dwell in the southern area were descendants of the refugees from Egypt; some of them, such as the Kenites, were not even Israelites at all. But the dominant group which gave the name "Judah" to the entire southern territory held tenaciously to the Egyptian tradition.

The most reasonable explanation is that this tradition, no matter how much it was later elaborated, has a substantial basis. There were Israelites who never were enslaved in Egypt: of that we can be certain. But there were also Israelites who looked back upon their liberation from Egypt as a great, divine deliverance.

If we inquire as to the period when it was most likely that a company of Israelites went to live in Egypt, we must answer about 1730 B.C., when the Hyksos or Desert

Kings (the Egyptians called them "Shepherd Kings") seized the rule of Egypt. The Hyksos, either related to the Hebrews or at least very friendly to them, would doubtless have welcomed the Israelite tribesmen to the Nile delta, if only for security reasons, and might even have elevated an Israelite to a position similar to the traditional one of Joseph. The story of Joseph as we have it in Genesis, however, we must regard as a kind of novel, parts of the plot of which have been borrowed from Egyptian folklore.[1]

It was never likely that the Hyksos would be able to maintain their reign. The probable reason for their initial success was a surprise weapon: the horse-drawn chariot, which they had developed in Canaan. From about 1580 to 1550 B.C., the Egyptians, through a succession of uprisings, expelled the Hyksos, many of whom undoubtedly returned to Canaan, probably taking groups of Israelites with them.

But evidently there were Israelites who remained. These, according to the book of Exodus, were forced into servitude and were used in the building of "store cities," Pithom and Raamses. Now these two cities have been excavated and we know the date of their construction. An inscription has also been found showing that heavy work was done by a people called 'Apiru, unquestionably the Hebrews. It would seem then that the oppression of the Israelites of Goshen was under Rameses II, and that the Exodus took place during the reign of his successor, Merneptah. This would give us a date of about 1230 B.C.

This date suits very well most of the archeological findings in southern Palestine, but not, as we have seen, the traditional dating of the fall of Jericho. If the Joshua whom the Pentateuch associates with Moses was the same Joshua who destroyed Jericho the Exodus would have to be put back a hundred years. Here the archeological evidence is conclusive. Jericho fell in the fourteenth century, before the Israelites under Moses had left Egypt. Or should the latter be the date to be revised? There are a

[1] See "The Tale of Two Brothers," in *Literature of the Ancient Egyptians*, by Adolf Erman, New York: E. P. Dutton & Co., Inc.; London: Nethven & Co., Ltd., 1927, pp. 150ff.

few scholars who think so. They point out that in the fourteenth century there was a period of confusion and upheaval in Egypt, exactly suited to the escape of the Israelites—which undoubtedly there was. There may indeed have been Israelites who did escape during this period. But it is difficult to identify them with those of the Exodus under Moses.

According to the Pentateuch, for instance, when the marching Israelites are ready to occupy positions east of the Jordan from which to mount their offensive into Canaan, they ask permission of the kings of Edom and Moab to use "the King's Highway," the familiar and convenient route that traverses their two countries on its way to Syria and the north. This permission is refused, requiring the Israelites to take a long and circuitous journey instead of one that would have been comparatively easy. Now here is the point to note: in the *thirteenth* century, the kingdoms of Edom and Moab were undoubtedly formidable and it is easy to believe that it was safer to march around them than to try to break through. But in the *fourteenth* century, a hundred years earlier, these kingdoms *did not exist,* and the area was in fact so sparsely populated that Moses and Joshua could have occupied it if they had wished without encountering the slightest resistance. This we know from one of the most complete archeological expeditions ever undertaken and it seems to show quite definitely, when added to the rest of the evidence, that the Exodus described in the Pentateuch did take place in the thirteenth rather than the fourteenth century, and that whatever "Joshua" took Jericho, he was not the Joshua who marched around Moab and Edom.[2]

Assuming then that the Exodus took place in the thirteenth century, how large was the company that Moses led from Egypt? Realistically, we must answer: a small one. The Bible story tells us that two midwives looked after the entire colony. This indicates a rather small community. But quite conclusive is the fact that the oases of the desert which are listed in the Pentateuch could not

[2] For the sake of avoiding too many complications, we are speaking of the fourteenth and thirteenth centuries, although the events attributed to the fourteenth occurred partly in the late fifteenth and those attributed to the thirteenth continued into the twelfth.

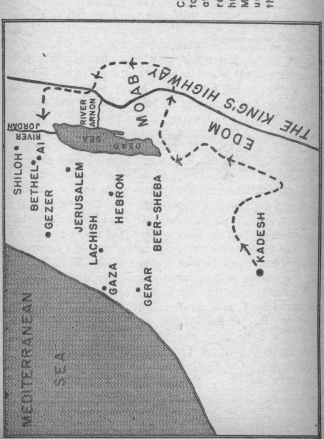

Circuitous route around MOAB taken by Israelites after permission refused to use king's highway. Since Moab did not exist until 13th century B.C., this tends to fix date.

MEDITERRANEAN SEA

SHILOH
BETHEL• •AI
•GEZER
JERUSALEM
LACHISH
GAZA• HEBRON
•GERAR BEER-SHEBA
•KADESH

RIVER JORDAN
RIVER ARNON

MOAB

EDOM

THE KING'S HIGHWAY

have supported a multitude but only such moderate numbers as they have always supported—unless we are to believe in "forty years" of daily miracle! The figures supplied in the Pentateuch are those of a misplaced census—doubtless the census taken by King David, to whose period they could reasonably belong. But they could not apply to the wanderings in the wilderness.

As the original company met and mingled with other tribes (as they are known to have done with the Kenites), the total, of course, would have become larger, as it also would by natural increase. But by this time the wandering Israelites had reached less desolate country.

Beneath the tradition, then, let us assume that there is this much solid history: that a company of oppressed Israelites escaped from Egypt under the leadership of one known as Moses in about 1230 B.C.; that they journeyed to Mount Sinai to make a covenant with the God of Moses; that at Sinai unusual events took place leaving a deep impress on their later history; that thereafter this company became mingled with other companies and finally formed a force strong enough to march east of the Jordan and conduct forays into the south of Palestine, as a result of which an Israelite settlement took place in which this group participated and which at last it dominated.

Broadly speaking, this is the view taken by modern scholars. But it leaves a number of important questions about the Hebrew settlement of Palestine which must still be considered.

2. Moses and Joshua

If (1) we could follow the traditional narrative without having to answer the questions it raises, and if (2) the traditional narrative were supported by archeological evidence and by inferences from later history, we would then be free to say that Joshua was first the associate of Moses, then his successor: the leader who took the Children of Israel across the Jordan into the Promised Land.

Perhaps someone named Joshua did indeed fill this role. But if so someone else to whom the Scriptures give the name of Joshua seems to have done quite a bit of conquering some considerable time before Moses was born. We have already seen that Jericho was destroyed a century before the campaign which followed the Exodus. This is a battle immemorially connected with the name of Joshua. Was there an earlier Joshua who organized the northern territory for Israelites who never knew Egyptian bondage and did he also invade the south as far as Jericho?

We notice that the Amarna tablets include letters to Pharaoh from the princes of Megiddo, Gezer, Askelon, Lachish, Jerusalem, and some other cities; but *none* from Shechem, Shiloh, Gibea, Mizpah and Jericho. Why? Was it not because the Israelites had already either destroyed or occupied these cities?

Tantalizingly, the Amarna tablets mention "Ya-shuya." Is this a "cuneiform" equivalent of "Joshua"? Scholars are uncertain. The name "Joshua" itself may be a later emendation of the name "Hosea"—and if not in the case of two persons who were thus named then perhaps in that of the first of them.

It is interesting to note that in the first chapter of the book of Judges the list of cities taken by the Israelites and those left undisturbed accords well with the evidence of the Amarna tablets: whereas the campaign which might be called that of "Second Joshua," the man who succeeded Moses, fits in remarkably well with the historical context suggested above.

Meanwhile we cannot avoid noticing that many years before the traditional "conquest" was supposed to have taken place, the city of Shechem gives every evidence of having become the established capital of the northern Israelite tribes. Most modern scholars believe that here, at Shechem, near Mount Gerizim, a confederacy of the Joseph tribes entered into a covenant and promulgated a code of laws. This code was based upon existing Canaanite codes, just as almost the entire culture of the northern tribes, from the alphabet onward, was based upon Canaanite culture.

Shechem had long been sacred to Jacob, whose other name was Israel. Here he had erected a pillar which he called "El-elohe-Yisrael," or "God, the God of Israel."

Here Joshua gave laws and enacted a covenant (Joshua xxiv; Deut. vii). So impressive is the place of Shechem in early Israelite history that many prominent scholars (including Holzinger, Steuernagel, Waterman, and, apparently, Meek) regard Shechem rather than Sinai as the shrine where the Book of the Covenant was transmitted.[3]

The Judean account of these matters was written much later and edited after the northern kingdom had ceased to be. What more natural than that the story should be changed to conform with the wishes—and traditions—of the surviving southern kingdom?

The cumulative evidence is impressive. We notice, for instance, in Genesis xxxviii, that "Judah," some centuries before the Exodus, is described as settling down in Canaan, intermarrying with the natives of the land. It sounds like a continuing history, not to be interrupted in the least by a sojourn in Egypt. We also observe that Ashur and Gad are the names of gods and it seems certain that these two tribes, although probably Hebrew, were quite independent until war—and the threat of further war—drew them into the confederation. To put the matter briefly, what we see is the gradual mingling of Hebrew communities with Canaanite and similar communities, sometimes peacefully, sometimes through violence and coercion; and all this had begun long before the traditional Exodus from Egypt.

To quote Professor T. J. Meek, a distinguished contemporary Old Testament scholar, "All the evidences, then, would seem to indicate quite definitely that there were Hebrews in Palestine, particularly in northern Palestine, all the time that there were Hebrews in Egypt and that only a comparatively small group ever went to Egypt."[4]

Professor Meek, joined by Professor A. T. Olmstead and others, definitely puts Joshua at least a century earlier than Moses and attributes to him the conquests that had taken place before the Israelites who had wandered with Moses in the wilderness crossed the Jordan. Since this

---

[3] The Book of the Covenant, closely connected with the Ten Commandments, is discussed in a later chapter.
[4] Theophile J. Meek, *Hebrew Origins*. New York: Harper & Brothers, 1936, p. 31.

earlier Joshua was also a law-giver, the question arises as to how much of what he did was later ascribed to Moses.

This we cannot answer, at least not with confidence, but it is apparent, as Professor Millar Burrows conjectures, that "a cycle of stories regarding a hero of the southern tribes, Moses, and another cycle about a northern hero, Joshua, might be combined after the tribes were united, and the dominance of the southern group might find expression in the representation of Joshua as attendant and successor of Moses."[5]

In the opinion of some scholars, the first Joshua's name was originally Hosea ("Salvation"), and he was a worshipper, not of Yahweh but of Canaanite gods and of El-elohe-Yisrael. The second Joshua, however, bore that name from the beginning ("Yahweh is salvation"), or at least from the time of a southern covenant with Yahweh. It would thus have been easy when Yahwistic editors changed Hosea's name to Joshua (to make it conform with the later Yahweh worship) to identify the two Joshuas in the Scriptures that were then being written, as though they had been one and the same person.

In any case, it is evident that the northern part of Palestine was settled by Israelites at least a century—probably more—before the south was, a fact of considerable importance, for in this length of time northern Israel was able to absorb Canaanite civilization, adopt its agricultural life, learn to follow its cults and worship its gods, and even develop its language into written Hebrew. Israel of the north was therefore considerably ahead of Judah of the south when the latter was established after the Exodus from Egypt. Only briefly were the two confederations ever united. When, after Solomon, they broke apart into separate kingdoms the division was final. Joshua's north and Moses' south could never really get together; but when the kingdom of the north had ended Judah of the south took over both traditions and wove them together, with a southern bias, into the "Books of Moses."

[5] *op. cit.*, p. 271.

3. Moses and Aaron

Having discovered that Joshua, the close associate of Moses in the traditional story, is separated from him by at least a hundred years, the reader may be in part prepared for the disclosure that Aaron, too, had little to do with his "brother," Moses. Not only is this indeed the case, but more startling still, Aaron may not even have been an historical person; he was, perhaps, no more than a literary invention.

In J—the oldest of the documents which are woven together to compose the Pentateuch—Aaron does not appear at all. In the E document, "he is clearly a supernumerary who was later introduced into the narrative as Israelite and Judean sagas became fused."[6]

If Aaron was to any extent historical he is to be identified with the bull worship which prevailed in the north throughout its entire history, even after the introduction of Yahweh (since in the north the worship of Yahweh was unquestionably connected with this image). As R. H. Kennett describes it, "The golden calf is [Aaron's]; he demands the materials of which it is made; he fashions it; and he presents it to the people, and dedicates it. Certainly, if any of the recorded acts of Aaron be historical, the episode of the golden calf can best claim to be so considered."[7] (Exod. xxxii: 2-6.)

It should be noted, perhaps, that in the Bible the word "calf" is used instead of "bull," but this is not because the image was actually that of a calf. It was that of a bull; but being much less than full size the word "calf" could be used of it by later writers (including the reforming prophets) contemptuously as a term of derision. The prophet Hosea, for instance (8th century), mockingly speaks of grown men who "kiss the calves" (Hos. xiii: 2). But the images were of bulls, not calves, and as we shall later see were connected with a fertility cult.

For what purpose then is "Aaron" introduced into the

6 Meek, *op. cit.*, p. 135.
7 R. H. Kennett, in *Journal of Theological Studies*, VI, p. 165. The present writer is on the whole drawn to the view that Aaron was fictional. But here there are no certainties.

narrative as a close associate of Moses—even as his "brother," in addition to being his spokesman and his chief priest? The answer is that during the long struggle for power between the various classes of Judean priests, it eventually became necessary for the metropolitan group that claimed exclusive rights to derive its sanction for these rights from the nation's founder, Moses. Originally, priests seem to have been drawn from any group whatever, according to the particular shrine they tended. Then, in the south, only Levites could be priests, and Levites had special privileges even in the north.[8]

There was also a priesthood descended from Zadok, the first high priest of Solomon's Temple in Jerusalem. There may or may not have been another claiming descent from "Aaron," the prototypical high priest of the north. Eventually, after the northern kingdom had been wiped out by the Assyrians, there was a movement for the centralizing of the worship of Yahweh in Jerusalem. This culminated in the publication of the Deuteronomic Code by King Josiah in 621 and the attempted abolition of all places of worship except the Temple at Jerusalem. The priests who were thus dispossessed of their shrines were given the right to officiate at the central sanctuary; provision was also made for their economic support. But neither arrangement proved feasible, and so it became necessary to reduce these provincial priests, the numerous descendants of the ancient Levites, to a lower order.

Naturally, all this was not done without a struggle; but after the fall of Jerusalem in 586 B.C. had put an end for a time to worship at Jerusalem new provisions were worked out during the Exile in Babylon which were inserted in the Priestly Code (document P). For reasons that are not clear to us but which, undoubtedly, were political, the select class of priests, in elevating itself above the rest of the Levites, chose to claim descent from a first high priest, the northern "Aaron," whom Yahweh (it was said) had himself appointed to this exalted office, and whom he

[8]Alternatively, the Levites may have been the priests of Yahweh wherever Yahweh was worshipped, sometimes, however, combining with Yahweh's worship (or absorbing to it) the worship of Canaanite gods. The question never rests on firm ground. The history of the Israelite priesthood is one of obscurity.

had made coadjutor and spokesman of his "brother," Moses. Perhaps the northern "Aaron" was chosen (the northern kingdom being defunct) to avoid rival claims in the south. Or perhaps he was invented. In any case, the narrative in the Pentateuch was amended accordingly!

But its contradictions were not smoothed out and not enough was done to make it self-consistent. In Deuteronomy the sons of Levi still have wide privileges, which in the book of Numbers are sharply cut down. As Pfeiffer puts it, "a few of the priests' campaign pamphlets found their way into the Pentateuch as supplements to the Priestly Code."[9] In this way, the priests became an exclusive caste; and the Levites, who had once all been priests, were reduced to a lower rank, servants of the priests, divested of almost all their former privileges.

To sum up, then: it was to gain impressive sanction for this "reform" that the priestly editors of the Pentateuch built up the insignificant Aaron into an important figure (or invented him) and found for him an exalted place only slightly less than that of Moses.[10] Thus the need of the later centuries rewrote the history of the earlier ones.

But actually Moses and Aaron (assuming that the latter existed) never met! They belong to diverse provinces of Hebrew religious culture, Moses to the south, Aaron to the north. Only in the sacred literature are they brought together when the schemes of priests make necessary an innovation in the national saga.

4. Moses and the Levites

At one time, as we have already seen, the Levites had exclusive rights—or very nearly so—to be the priests of Yahweh in Judah. Apparently, they had almost the same rights, so far as the worship of Yahweh was concerned, in northern Israel, too. Who were the Levites?

If we follow the tradition they were the descendants

---

9 Pfeiffer, *op. cit.*, p. 795. See his section on "Prerogatives of the Clergy" (pp. 792-801) for an excellent condensed discussion of this struggle.
10 The name "Aaron" is similar to the name for "Ark" ("aron"). Perhaps he was "personalized" out of the Ark tradition, a plausible theory but not without its difficulties.

of Levi, one of the sons of Jacob, and therefore one of the twelve tribes of Israel. But if so why was no portion of the "Promised Land" assigned to them? If the answer is that they were the official priesthood whose province it was to dwell with *all* the tribes, the question then becomes, At what time and under what conditions did it happen so?

It is a striking fact that only the Levites among the tribes of Israel bear Egyptian names. Phinehas, Hur, Hophni, Pashur, Putiel, Merari, Assir—these are Egyptian names and also the names of Levites. Moses is a Levite; and his, too, is an Egyptian name—and one which does *not* mean "drawn from the water," as the traditional explanations have so piously maintained. It means "a child given"—usually by a god. (Thus "Amon-mose" means "Amon has given a child.") His actual name, of course, was not Moses; the final "s" is given in Greek (in the Septuagint) to make the name pronounceable. In Hebrew, it is *Mosheh;* but actually, it is none of these but the Egyptian, *mesu* or *mose,* a child.[11]

But even so, it is not really a name: as it stands it is only part of a name, incomplete. It must originally have been Ptah-mose or Aton-mose or there must have been some other prefix indicating the divinity whose "theophorous" child he was supposed to be. This part of his name has been either lost or suppressed. So what we have is merely "child-of-," and to this we have become accustomed without knowing that it lacks the most important element of its meaning.

However, what is most relevant to us is the fact that Moses is described in the Pentateuch as a Levite, and we see that, like many other Levites, he bears an Egyptian name (or part of a name). It is also remarkable that in not a single instance is an Egyptian name found among the other tribes. When, having noticed this, we also notice the close relationship of the Levites to Moses, as described in the Sinai episode, it is strongly suggested to us that it may have been the Levi tribe—and perhaps *only* the Levi tribe—that Moses led out of Egypt.

11 Gr. LXX: usually Μωυσῆς; occasionally Μωσῆς; Hebrew נבשׁה . See James H. Breasted, *The Dawn of Conscience,* New York: Charles Scribner's Sons, 1934, p. 350.

Many scholars have accepted this view and go on to suppose that, later, in the wilderness, the Levi tribe was federated with other tribes that had not been enslaved in Egypt and became the priests of the entire confederation. But if so, of what cult were they priests? That this cult, whatever it was, included the serpent as a god of healing and fertility cannot be doubted. Moses made such a "brazen serpent" in the wilderness (Num. xxi: 5-9), one that was eventually (and rather unsentimentally) destroyed in the reform of King Hezekiah five hundred years later. The name "Levi" is itself related to the serpent (Arabic: *lawah,* to twist or coil) and to *Levi*athan, the dragon god of the primordial myths as well as a deity of later times. A number of Levite names are formed from words meaning "snake," and it is known from archeological findings that the serpent fertility cult had many adherents in Palestine during the centuries of Israelite occupation.[12]

What we seem to have down to now, therefore, is a serpent-fertility cult in Judea paralleling a bull-fertility cult in northern Israel, the former being connected with the Levites and the latter with Aaron. But in this case what becomes of the worship of Yahweh? It is true that Yahweh could eventually be worshipped through the bull image and the serpent image—and indeed most certainly was—but insofar as he is met with the wilderness it is undoubtedly as a thunder-god and perhaps as a volcano-god, and his concern is with war rather than with fertility. What then was the relationship of the Levites—and of Moses—to "Yahweh of Hosts," the Sinai-Midian God of War?

It is at this point that the reader must be given more plainly to understand that in the thirteenth century B.C., and indeed for many centuries later, we are *not yet dealing with monotheism,* the worship of only one God. Because the Pentateuch has been largely edited to a much later viewpoint it looks superficially as though the Israelites were called to the worship of Yahweh and of Yahweh alone, even in the wilderness, and that it was from this as a clearly stated requirement of the Covenant that they repeatedly fell away.

---

12 The evidence is summarized by Meek, *op. cit.* chap. 4. See also G. H. Skipwith, *Jewish Quarterly Review*, XI, pp. 264ff.

No scholar believes this today. The Scriptures themselves are full of the evidence that gods other than Yahweh were worshipped and without any thought in those early days that Yahweh had ever made an exclusive claim. Not until Elijah at the very earliest (9th century B.C.) is the existence of other gods, and their right to be worshipped, called into question. It is therefore perfectly possible that the Levites were connected with a serpent-fertility cult and at the same time undertook some special function when a covenant was made with Yahweh. Moses himself, even according to the traditional story, had no difficulty in harmonizing the special claims of Yahweh with those of the god represented by the brazen serpent. (We postpone for the moment the theory that the two became identical.) Just as, much later, King Solomon, having erected a temple to Yahweh as the national shrine of all Israel, proceeded to erect temples to other deities on opposite hillsides of his capital city of Jerusalem. The writer of the books of Kings frowns upon the proceeding, it is true, but he was writing much later than the event.

Of this, however, we shall see more in a subsequent chapter. For the present it is enough to notice that Moses, whatever in the Hebrew Scriptures he eventually became, was first of all, so far as we can see, the leader of the Levites, and almost certainly it was they, and they alone, whom he delivered from captivity in Egypt. Nevertheless, there are other views, and we shall have to consider them.

5. *Freud's View of Moses*

According to Sigmund Freud, the father of modern psychology, Moses was not a Hebrew but an Egyptian. Bitterly reproached for setting forth this thesis, Freud replies that he did not arrive at it lightheartedly. If he, a Jew, had adopted an opinion which denied to the Jewish people "the man whom it praises as the greatest of its sons," it is because he had refused "to set aside truth in favor of supposed national interest."[13]

[13]Sigmund Freud, *Moses and Monotheism.* New York: Alfred A. Knopf, Inc., 1939, p. 1.

Using psychoanalytical techniques, critics of Freud have detected in him anti-Semitic and other morbid factors which are responsible, they think, for his abandonment of Moses to the Egyptians. We cannot concern ourselves with these matters here; nor can we be deterred by Freud's own warning that he will not be well understood except by the few who are skilled in psychoanalysis. We shall have to assume that Freud's viewpoint either does or does not fit the historical situation and that it either could or could not be true. There can be no doubt at all of its relevance. This we accept. But we shall examine it, not psychoanalytically, which is beyond our competence and the purpose of this book, but historiographically.

To Freud, Moses has an Egyptian name for the simple reason that he is an Egyptian. The myth of his being cradled in the reeds by the riverside he interprets as other such myths have long since been interpreted and arrives at the view that Moses was of noble birth and exercised the prerogatives of high station. He was a devoted admirer and disciple of Ikhnaton, the famous pharaoh who for the first time in history established monotheism: the worship of one God only, whose symbol was the sun and whose name was Aton. With this faith went high ethical standards but also religious intolerance. Non-existent gods must not be worshipped, and the evils done in their name must be wiped out.

After the death of Ikhnaton, his reforms were swiftly swept away. Moses, deeply disappointed and realizing that his own people, the Egyptians, had rejected a high and pure religion, looked for another people, one that he hoped would accept it. He chose the Israelites of Goshen.

We will note in passing that there is nothing inherently improbable in Freud's theory down to now, except that, unless we give up the 1230 B.C. date for the Exodus, Moses could not have been a contemporary of Ikhnaton but would need to have lived a century later. Freud, who prefers the fourteenth-century date, nevertheless allows that the later date may be correct, and meets objections by pointing out, quite satisfactorily, that heresies do not die easily and that Ikhnaton's followers undoubtedly formed a school, secret or open, which continued to communicate his doctrines. Moses, in this event, belonged to Ikhnaton's school and was fervently concerned to carry to success its interrupted purpose.

Is there any other evidence for this approach? According to the famous Jewish historian, Josephus (first century A.D.), Moses was the "Egyptian" general who commanded the armies that overwhelmed Ethiopia (in Hebrew, "Cush"). Also according to Josephus (*Antiquities*, Bk. II, Chap. x), Moses took an Ethiopian wife at the close of this campaign, which accords readily with the Bible's story of Miriam and Aaron[14] complaining against Moses "because of the Cushite (Ethiopian) woman he had married: for he had married a Cushite woman" (Num. xii: 1). What effect Moses' Cushite marriage had upon his marriage with Zipporah, the Midianite, and upon her "leaving" him and then "returning" to him under the guardianship of her father, Jethro (or Reuel, which was he?), it is difficult to say. But at any rate, from such circumstances, Freud's viewpoint gains some plausibility.

Having persuaded the Israelites that he will lead them in making a solemn compact with the one and only God, Aton, Moses and his following go out into the wilderness. Here Freud makes a great point of the Israelites being compelled by Moses to accept the Egyptian rite of circumcision. That circumcision was an Egyptian rite, and not originally Hebraic, will have to be conceded. None of the Semitic tribes at that time practiced circumcision; but the Egyptians did, and were contemptuous of all who did not.

It will nevertheless have to be noted that according to another Scriptural tradition it was Joshua who instituted circumcision[15] at Gibeath-ha-araloth (misconstrued in the Bible story as "The Hill of Foreskins"), after which Yahweh exclaims, "This day have I rolled away the reproach of Egypt from off you" (Jos. v: 9). Which can only mean

---

14 Whether Aaron was historical or not is irrelevant when we are seeking only the facts to which stories about him may be pointing, half hidden by tradition.

15 Which would have been unnecessary if, upon the basis of the traditional interpretation, the Mosaic ritual had been carried out in the wilderness —but of course, the Scriptures that prescribe it did not exist until centuries later.

that the Egyptians could no longer taunt the Israelites with the physical sign of their inferiority. The Israelites were now anatomically equal with the Egyptians. But who instituted the rite—Joshua or Moses?

At this point we naturally think of the strange story, mentioned when we were summarizing the traditional narrative, in which Moses is savagely attacked by Yahweh because he has not been circumcised. This, says Freud, is "a deliberate contradiction of the significant truth," meaning, apparently, that in this fragment an attempt is made to suppress the Egyptian nationality of Moses by showing dramatically that he could not have been an Egyptian since he was not circumcised; and at the same time (paradoxically) emphasizing that he was a Hebrew by making the Hebrew deity require his circumcision as a *Hebrew* institution.

Perhaps so; but most scholars have had to leave this story in the same dark obscurity in which they found it. It is enough, however, that Freud shows that the Israelites who left Egypt under Moses for some reason seem to have accepted the Egyptian rite of circumcision, one which eventually prevailed throughout all Israel.

Moses took his following to Mount Sinai, the site of Egyptian copper mines, and also the birthplace, as is now supposed, of the alphabet.[16] Was there in this unlikely place a small center of cosmopolitan culture? Excavation has revealed that there probably was. It might have happened (and this Freud did not know) that a group of Ikhnaton followers at Sinai, protected by distance and by the forbidding bleakness of the desert from the heresy-hunting priests of Egypt, were still engaged in the worship of Aton in all its original idealistic fervor and intolerant rigidity. It may be that among these compatriots Moses found wisdom and encouragement for his venture.

To remain with Freud, however, and summarizing sharply his interpretation, at some point there came to be a violent disagreement between Moses and the leaders of the people, perhaps because Moses, like Ikhnaton before him, was imposing his monotheism too imperiously. (The Bible says he had his Levites kill three thousand Israelites

16 See Burrows, *op. cit.*, pp. 180ff.

for apostasy, Exod. xxxii: 28.) But at any rate, says Freud, Moses was killed and the people moved from Sinai to Midian. Here they accepted the volcano-god, Yahweh (there are no volcanoes, extinct or otherwise, at Sinai; there are in Midian), who was a cloud by day and a pillar of fire by night, and this was the God of War who eventually led them into Canaan.

But Moses is not forgotten. In the conscience of the people the crime against him murmurs its reproach. Eventually, in the voices of the prophets, it cries aloud. After hundreds of years of worshipping false gods and bowing before idols the Children of Israel finally acknowledge Moses and accept his monotheism. And the Scriptures that tell the story are changed and altered so that Moses seems to have been the accepted leader all along.

There is much more, of course, to the Freudian view of Moses than can be developed in a treatment as brief as this—involving, according to Freud's own requirement, a working knowledge of psychoanalysis (!). Let the reader, if he is attracted to it, consider the matter further in Freud's own essays.[17] But meanwhile let us notice that historically it is not necessary for Moses to have been an Egyptian in order to have been attracted to the doctrines of Ikhnaton. He could very well have been an Israelite with an Egyptian education who said to himself, "If the Egyptians find this religion too hard for them, we will prove that it is not too hard for Israel." If, as seems almost certain, he was a Levite (if he was not an Egyptian), his people were doubtless followers of a serpent god. What he had to do in this case was to persuade them to follow the one true God whose Egyptian name was Aton but who, for Israelites, would have had to have a Hebrew name. How might he have attempted it?

Since, in discussing this question, we can appropriately take our leave of Freud, let us consider it on its own merits in a separate section.

17See footnote, p. 57. It should be noted that for Biblical criticism, Freud depends upon German scholars whose views are not to be taken lightly. On the other hand, these critics are not to be regarded as accepting the views set forth by Freud. Many scholars have been much interested by the arguments Freud adduces but few have confessed themselves convinced.

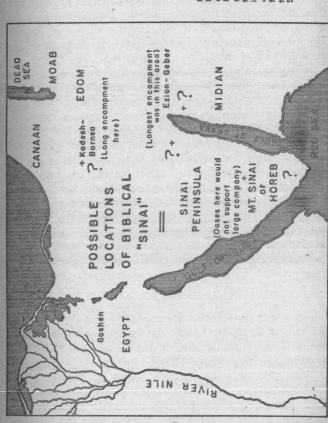

POSSIBLE LOCATIONS OF BIBLICAL "SINAI"

CANAAN

DEAD SEA

MOAB

EDOM

+ Kadesh-Barnea
? (Long encampment here)

Goshen

EGYPT

RIVER NILE

SINAI PENINSULA

(Oases here would not support large company)
+
MT. SINAI or HOREB
?

(Longest encampment was in this area)
? +
? +
Ezion-Geber

GULF OF SUEZ

MIDIAN

RED SEA

In addition to the locations shown, at one or more of which Moses may have given "The Law" to some of the tribes, it is possible that Joshua gave the first 'Law' (Book of the Covenant) at Shechem in Canaan.

6. The God of Sinai and the God of Midian

Before tracing the possibility that it was a monotheist doctrine that Moses taught to the Israelites who gathered at Mount Sinai, we must face the fact that we do not know where the Biblical Mount Sinai was. We know, of course, the mountainous region to which this name is given on our maps, and we know that the route described in Exodus appears to take the Children of Israel to this location. But we have to admit that the description may be wrong and that the Mount Sinai of the Bible—or Mount Horeb: both names are used—may have been near the northern end of the Gulf of Akaba, in Midian.

It was in Midian, according to the Pentateuch, that Yahweh first revealed himself to Moses. Jethro, by whom Moses was employed and whose daughter he married, appears to have been a priest of Yahweh, a god of Midian. The once volcanic mountains of this area are exactly suited to the description of "a pillar of cloud by day and of fire by night," whereas, as we have noted, there are no volcanoes, either active or extinct, in the southern part of the peninsula at the geographical Mount Sinai. Moreover, it seems certain that the Israelites from Egypt spent many years in the Midian area, whereas it is entirely conjectural as to whether they were ever in the traditional Mount Sinai vicinity at all.

Nevertheless it is difficult to see why the tradition ever indicated the southern location, charting the journey of the Israelites, stage by stage, until they reached it, if there is no basis for it. Here we shall assume—since an assumption one way or the other is necessary—that the Israelites led out of Egypt by Moses did indeed assemble before Mount Sinai, and that afterwards they went on to Midian —quite possibly without Moses.

What then was the doctrine taught by Moses? What God did he seek to make known to the people at Sinai? That monotheism was possible to the Israelites at this early date has long been denied. We can trace the development of Semitic religion from primitive animism through polytheism and henotheism to the eventual monotheism of the late period much more naturally if we suppose that the heralds of monotheism were the Hebrew prophets; but the latter were many centuries in the future; how could monotheism be possible to Moses?

The answer (for which we do not need Freud's thesis) may very well be Ikhnaton. Monotheism *was* achieved, and *before* the time of Moses, and there is no reason whatever for supposing that all memory of it had been extinguished. According to Albright,[18] in the period from 1500 to 1200 B.C. there was a tendency towards monotheism not only in Egypt but throughout Western Asia. The intermixing of cultures and the increased facility in international communications, were giving rise to syncretism in religious conceptions. Different gods with the same function were being fused together; local gods were beginning to be thought of (though not with logical consistency) as manifestations of a single deity whose rule was not restricted by locality.

Now it so happens that in Egyptian liturgics at the time of Moses there was a formula concerning the supreme God, the Creator, that was very well known and went as follows: "He who causes to exist what comes into existence." Translated into Hebrew, this becomes "Yahweh-asher-yihweh," of which YHWH (Yahweh) is an abbreviation.[19] It may very well be, therefore, that Moses tried to bring about a "covenant" between the Israelites from Egypt and the Universal God whom he knew in Egyptian as Aton and in Hebrew as Yahweh.

But, if so, what happened? Did he fail? Did the Israelites return to their previous gods? Did Moses order a massacre as recorded in Exodus xxxii, and did the intended victims resist and was Moses killed in the struggle? We cannot answer these questions but we can be sure that between the conception of Yahweh as a Universal God, which we are here for the moment attributing to Moses, and Yahweh as he appears in Midian there is a vast gulf

18 William F. Albright, *The Archeology of Palestine and the Bible*. New York: Fleming H. Revell Company, 1935, pp. 165ff.
19 Albright, *op. cit.*, pp. 164 and 217. Meek, *op. cit.*, pp. 99ff. Also, for a full discussion, G. R. Driver, *Zeitschrift für die alttestamentliche Wissenschaft*, XLVI.

of divergence. Though the name is the same they are two different gods.

Yahweh of Midian is a tempestuous, unpredictable, despotic god, who is unreasonable and loses his temper and has to be cajoled into acting with civilized restraint. He is a god of thunder and his name may mean "the One who Blows." The possibilities in the name Yahweh (with its variants, Yah, Yahu, Hawah, etc.) are immense. Was it because of the extreme ambiguity of the name that it could be used both for the God of Moses at Sinai and the god of Jethro at Midian? Provided the monotheism of Moses actually existed, there is no better solution. Yahweh of Sinai, the Universal God, somehow became Yahweh of Midian, the Israelite war-god, during the years that the Children of Israel wandered in the wilderness.

It may be that it was only Levites that Moses led out of Egypt, as we have already strongly conjectured. Other tribes may swiftly have added themselves, even before the encampment at Mount Sinai. These tribes, like the Levites earlier, may have agreed to enter into a Covenant. The Covenant may have required that they become "a kingdom of priests and a holy nation," just as the story in Exodus provides; this would mean that they would be missionaries of the one true God, to whom they were unreservedly dedicated. But the Covenant may have proved too much for the added tribes, so that only the Levites remained faithful to it. This would explain the command of Moses to the Levites to punish with death those who had broken their vows. And Moses may indeed—in a more than literal sense—have shattered the "stone tablets" upon which the Covenant had been inscribed. Like Ikhnaton, he may have been intolerant, eager to enforce his monotheism, and so in an enraged moment may have given the order for a massacre—the one that, necessarily, the tribes resisted. Thereafter, afraid to let him rule them any longer, they may have carried him up his mountain and put him to death. Was this the "sin" that later tradition was unwilling to reveal—and which cut him off from the "Promised Land"?

This would explain why "no man knoweth of his sepulchre." Certainly it is unthinkable that if Moses were still the Israelite leader when Mount Nebo was reached—the revered leader who gave his final exhortations and his blessing to his beloved followers before he died—he would be allowed to be buried in an unmarked grave. It would be known from the instant of his death that his sepulchre would be a place of pilgrimage. We can only suppose, therefore, that (upon the basis of this theory) whether in the circumstances we have conjectured or in some other circumstances, the Moses who led the Levites out of Egypt perished near the time of Sinai; and that another leader, one whom tradition would identify with Moses, led the tribes to Midian and to the Covenant with the Midianite Yahweh.

Perhaps after the death of Moses, the Levites, in order to bring peace to the tribes, made a compromise that restored their old god, the brazen serpent. But they may have secretly retained—and finally have brought to triumph—the tradition that made Moses the dominant leader: the deliverer who brought "the Children of Israel out of Egypt," the "servant of Yahweh," the one true God.

There are scholars who believe they see in the writing of the prophets, and particularly of Hosea, veiled references to the fate of Moses. If there was indeed so active a tradition, monotheism, however much obscured, was a factor in the life of Israel from the very beginning. But we cannot be sure of it. On the contrary, having developed the monotheistic theory of the work of Moses as far as it is possible (in a brief treatment) to develop it, we must now consider the opposite and—according to most scholars—more probable possibility: that Moses was the leader who made the Covenant with Yahweh of Midian, and that monotheism had no place in it.[20] This, we repeat, is the conclusion arrived at by the majority of scholars; and fortunately it does not need to be proved true or false in order to become the starting point for a sufficient understanding of the gradual development by which Israel

---

20 It is no part of our intention to press any one theory to the exclusion of others. The only interpretative principle to which we are committed is that of the natural evolution of religious concepts, of which the religion of Israel is illustrative and typical. On this basis, any of the several theories we are considering would fit our eventual conclusion.

did arrive at the worship of a Universal Lord, an image-less God whose requirement was not sacrifice but right-eousness.

7. *How Much Is Certain?*

The confederation of the southern Israelite tribes may have taken place at Sinai, at Ezion-Geber on the Gulf of Akaba, or at Kadesh in the Wilderness of Sin. Codes of law including one or more series of Ten Commandments may have been given them at any of these places (or by Joshua at Canaan). Moses may have been the leader after Sinai or he may not. There may never have been an encampment at Sinai.

These are the uncertainties, fascinating to investigate but impossible to resolve. There are, however, some certainties, and it is upon these that our understanding of the religion of Israel eventually must rest. We know, for instance, that the northern part of Palestine was settled by Hebrews who were never enslaved in Egypt and who entered Canaan more than a century before Moses. These Israelites, although they may have had their own tribal gods, in the main adopted the religion of the Canaanites, gradually making room for the Judaic national God, Yahweh.

It is scarcely to be doubted that in the south, too, many Israelite settlers knew nothing of Egyptian bondage. But a group of tribes, Kenite and perhaps Midianite as well as Israelite, had formed a federation in the wilderness, the strongest tribe (or the one that eventually became so) being Judah.[21] The priests of the federated tribes were the Levites who had been led by Moses out of Egypt. The tribal deity was a god of war, Yahweh, who was carried—according to tradition—enthroned above an "Ark of the Covenant" wherever the tribes wandered and who eventually was enshrined in a temple at Jerusalem. He may,

[21]This may seem inconsistent with the earlier statement that the tribe of Judah may have settled in Canaan a century or more before the Exodus. But we do not know how much of the tribe of Judah was involved. Even if the wilderness confederation did not include Judah at all (because Judah was already resident in Canaan) there is no doubt that in Canaan itself Judah gained complete ascendancy—but in the process adopted the Sinai tradition, perhaps through the Levite priests.

however, have combined his warlike character with the
requirements of a fertility cult, in which case his symbol
was the serpent, encased *within* the ark.

The Judah tribes, like their northern neighbors, worshipped not only Yahweh but the gods of Canaan. Yet
between Israel in the north and Judah in the south there
were significant differences. Yahweh was the god of Judah
to an extent that he never was of Israel; and the brief
unification under David and Solomon did not suffice to
give to Yahweh-worship in the north the acceptance it had
gained in the south. Two traditions sprang up and were
developed separately although not unrelated to each other.
There were also many traditions associated with wells and
springs, trees and stone pillars; local gods could be worshipped at many sacred places. Both north and south, a
literature began to appear, depicting the respective national sagas. When the northern kingdom was finally destroyed (721 B.C.) its literature was taken over by Judah
in the south and edited—though imperfectly—to conform
to southern standards and traditions. When Jerusalem was
destroyed (586 B.C.) and its leading citizens transported
into Babylon, the literature was again edited and the
Judaic law, now attributed to Moses, was worked out
afresh and codified. With the restoration of national life
(now to be called Jewish) in the southern area (now
Judea) from the late sixth to the middle of the fifth centuries B.C., the existing Scriptures took almost their final
form, though more were later to be added; and it is this
entire period that we must keep in mind—from the thirteenth to the fourth centuries B.C.—as we turn to the Ten
Commandments.

CHAPTER FOUR

The Riddle of the Ten Words

1. The Three Standard Arrangements

Correctly translated, the Hebrew of the Bible does not say "Ten Commandments" but "Ten Words." Turned into Greek this gives us the term *Decalogue,* a precise rendering of the original Hebrew. It is as the Decalogue that the famous code has long been known to scholars—as it has to a great extent in ordinary parlance—and this is the term we shall now most often use as we proceed with our discussion.

Unfortunately, the arrangement of the Decalogue is not the same in all communions. The first sentence—"I am the Lord thy God, which brought thee out of the land of Egypt, out of the house of bondage"—is counted a preface by the Greek and Reformed Churches, as it is by the Roman Catholic and Lutheran; but in the Jewish communion it is counted, not unreasonably, as the First Word or "Commandment." The prohibition, "Thou shalt have no other gods before me," is given as the First Commandment in the Greek and Reformed Churches but is combined with the prohibition of "graven images" by the Roman Catholic and Lutheran Churches to make one Commandment (the First), whereas in the Jewish communion the same combination of the two prohibitions makes the Second Commandment.

The Greek, Reformed and Jewish Commandments Three to Nine become the Roman Catholic and Lutheran Two to Eight, and the Tenth Commandment of the former group is divided into two by the latter. But the division is not quite the same: the Roman Catholic Ninth Commandment protects in the first place the neighbor's wife, the Lutheran, his house.

In the Septuagint, the second-century translation of the Hebrew Scriptures into Greek,[1] the order of the Commandments is changed, Commandments Five and Seven being brought together and the Commandment we know as the Sixth being given as the Eighth. These are not earth-shaking divergences, but they allow us to see at the outset how difficult it is to "standardize" the Decalogue, and warn us, perhaps, of more disturbing discoveries that lie ahead. Before coming to these, we shall remind ourselves once more that there are two versions of the Decalogue, one in Exodus—the one with which we are more familiar—and another in Deuteronomy. We shall consider the Deuteronomic version first, since we know that it was written before the one in Exodus.[2]

2. The Decalogue in Deuteronomy

The word "Deuteronomy," the title of the fifth and last book of the Pentateuch, results from a mistranslation (Deut. xvii: 18) from Hebrew into Greek. It means "Second Law," thereby implying that a "First Law" had already been promulgated. *This implication we must put completely out of mind*.[3] It is true that in this book, Moses is portrayed as recapitulating a great deal that has been set forth in the previous (*not* earlier) books, including the Decalogue, but it is also true that the "recapitulation" is in the language of the seventh century B.C. The supposedly earlier legislation appearing in Exodus, Leviticus and Numbers is from the Priestly Code

---

[1] See p. 17.

[2] There is still a further version of the Decalogue on a fragment known as the Nash Papyrus, dated about 100 B. C. Its variations are not, however, sufficiently significant to require consideration in the present rather general discussion.

[3] In place of the traditional assumptions, we must have constantly in view the basic information developed in an earlier chapter. The books and chapters of the Bible were *not* written in the order in which they appear, and this is true of the Pentateuch. The first chapter of Genesis, for instance, was one of the latest to be written. In each of the five books, early and late material is woven together, but most though by no means all of Deuteronomy was composed in the same period and by a single writer.

which was compiled later than most of Deuteronomy, in the sixth and fifth centuries, during the Exile in Babylon. During this same period, the entire Pentateuch, including Deuteronomy, was extensively edited and revised.

The Deuteronomist, who was almost certainly a priest of the Temple at Jerusalem, has a quite distinctive style that is easily identified even where he writes only a few sentences. S. R. Driver long ago made a list of the words and phrases used by him and by no one else in the Bible. A few examples are the following: "a mighty hand and a stretched-out arm"; "the land whither thou goest in to possess it"; "with all your heart and with all your soul"; "that it may be well with thee"; "to do that which is right in the eyes of Yahweh"; "a peculiar people." Because of his singularities of style, we almost always know when we are reading the Deuteronomist.

When did his book appear? Unquestionably his was the book discovered in the Temple by the Judaic king, Josiah, in 621 B.C. (II Kings, xxii). It was not as large then as it is now, and it had not been so many times revised. But essentially it was the same book. Upon the basis of this book, Josiah instituted his far-reaching reforms, extinguishing all other worship than that of Yahweh and centralizing the cultus of the latter in the Temple at Jerusalem. The book and the reforms belong together, and both belong to the prophetic movement that began in the preceding century.

In this connection it is interesting that in the Lachish letters, found in the ashes left from the conflagration of 588 B.C., which are dated after Josiah's reform, archeologists have noticed the sudden absence of theophorous personal names that include the syllable, "Baal." The names are now all Yahweh names (Yahu). Josiah's reform had carried out the mandate of the Deuteronomic code and Yahweh had become the foremost—perhaps the only—God of Judah.

In Deuteronomy the Decalogue is found in chapter v. Of the lesser differences between this version and that in Exodus, those worth noting are the following: (1) in the Fifth Commandment, Exodus connects long life with the duty of honoring the father and the mother and does not speak of any other recompense, whereas the Deuteronomist adds "that it may go well with thee upon the land which Yahweh, thy God, giveth thee." (2) In the Tenth Commandment, the Deuteronomist warns first against coveting one's neighbor's wife, where Exodus gives "house," and to the categories of things not to be coveted the Deuteronomist adds "field."

By far the most important difference, however, is in the Fourth Commandment. In Exodus the basis for sabbath observance is that God "made heaven and earth, the sea, and all that in them is, and rested the seventh day: wherefore the Lord blessed the sabbath day, and hallowed it." In Deuteronomy we have quite a different basis. The sabbath is to be observed "that thy manservant and thy maidservant may rest as well as thou. And thou shalt remember that thou wast a servant in the land of Egypt, and the Lord, thy God, brought thee out thence by a mighty hand and by a stretched-out arm: therefore the Lord, thy God, commanded thee to keep the sabbath day."

This is the Deuteronomist's humanitarianism. That he wrote this Commandment cannot be doubted. The style is his, and unmistakable. The ethical insight is that of the prophetic period when an outcry had been made in the name of Yahweh against injustice and oppression. Whatever, therefore, may be said of any other of the Commandments, this one the Deuteronomist has made his own. The sabbath was to be observed, not because it had been a rest-day of God and was therefore sacrosanct, but because human well-being was sacred and people who were tired deserved a rest.

The impossibility of ascribing this Commandment to Moses—or, in this form, to anyone other than the Deuteronomist—is at once apparent. Moreover, as we have noticed earlier, no one person could have given this Commandment and at the same time have given the one in Exodus. If the Commandments were ever on tables of stone, they must have appeared in one version or the other: but which was it? In fact, could it have been *either*?

In Exodus, as we saw, the narrative is not clear as to whether it was the Ten Commandments or another decalogue that was inscribed on the tables of stone. Deuter-

The famous Vatican statue of Moses by Michelangelo. The horns which appear in the statue are due to a mistranslation of Exodus xxxiv: 29, 30. The correct translation is that the skin of Moses' face "shone" (Hebrew: "sent forth beams"). In ancient Hebrew, the written word for "beams" and "horns" is the same.

The Bettmann Archive

Traditional depiction of Moses and the Tables of Stone on which are inscribed the Ten Commandments (Exodus version). Lithograph after a painting by Phillippe de Champaigne (17th Century).

Photo Ted Batchelor

Courtesy Paul Ilton

Stone snake from Gezer, Palestine, used in Canaanitish worship before 1200 B.C. This was found in a cave that was probably a worshipping place of early Canaanites. The Israelitish worship of a Bronze Serpent, said to have been made by Moses, was a related cult; King Hezekiah destroyed the Bronze Serpent in the 8th century B.C.

Ramses II, the Pharaoh who put the Israelites to oppressive tasks.

Hammurabi receiving the Tables of the Law from the Sun God, Shamesh. The Old Testament Law was in part derived from the Code of Hammurabi. Recent archeological discoveries have required the re-dating of Hammurabi's reign from the 20th to the 17th century, B.C. Moses lived four centuries later.

Ikhnaton (Amenophis IV) from whom monotheism of Moses could, on some hypotheses, have been derived. 18th Dynasty, 1370 B.C.

Queen Nofretete, wife of Ikhnaton (Amenophis IV), 18th Dynasty, 1375 B.C.

onomy says plainly that it was the Ten Commandments—in its own version! "These words," Moses is caused to say, "Yahweh spake unto all your assembly in the mount out of the midst of the fire, and of the cloud, and of the thick darkness, with a great voice: and he added no more. And he wrote them upon two tables of stone, and gave them unto me" (Deut. v: 22).

This, however, is mere legendary ascription, since it is quite conclusive that the Fourth Commandment was written not by Moses but by the Deuteronomist. In the Exodus version it was rewritten by the compilers of the Priestly Code. What we have, therefore, in the Ten Commandments is a code developed over a period of time. How long this period was and whether it began with Moses we still may ask; but Mosaic authorship itself is no more possible than that the stones were inscribed by the finger of God. The Commandments, like other great codes, emerged in the course of a natural, social evolution.

3. The Decalogue in Exodus

It will be remembered that when we tried to tell the traditional story of the Ten Commandments, following the Sinai narrative exactly as it is given in the book of Exodus, we reached a point of complete frustration. Moses had several times descended the mountain and spoken with the people; yet when he came down with the tables of stone it was as though these earlier visits had never taken place. The people had grown tired even of wondering what had become of him and had given him up for lost.

Again, when the second set of tables of stone are inscribed, the first having been broken by Moses, it is an entirely different decalogue that is given (Exod. xxxiv), and it is this other decalogue that is described as the law of the Covenant.

On the traditional basis, as we saw, these problems could not be resolved. But a solution is at once in sight when we turn to scholarly analysis and separate the various elements that compose the book of Exodus *according to their sources*. For we discover that we are not dealing with a continuous narrative, written all at the same time; we are dealing with fragments, of varying ages, put together by editors and repeatedly re-edited.

Upon this basis we now see that the Ten Commandments are *an insertion,* breaking the connection between the end of Exodus xix and the continuation of the story in chapter xx (18ff.). If the reader will take a copy of the Bible and look up these passages, he will see for himself, even with nothing more than the English translation to guide him, how abruptly the Decalogue breaks into the narrative.

That the context into which the Decalogue is forced is older than the Decalogue itself is obvious. It is a case of a more recently developed code being thrust into the framework of an older one. As to the age at which the Exodus Decalogue could have been written, it cannot be earlier than 500 B.C. Before that time, for instance, the clause in the Fourth Commandment relating that "in six days Yahweh made heaven and earth, the sea, and all that in them is, and rested the seventh day" could not have been written. It is based upon the creation myth in Genesis i (Document P), which was composed during the Exile.

Whether the Decalogue in a simpler form might be much older is a very different question. Commandments Six to Nine are in short sentences; might the other Commandments at one time have been similarly brief? Certainly a shorter form would have been more suitable for engraving upon stone. Is it possible then that the Decalogue as we now have it is a more elaborate form of an ancient code that was composed of ten short clauses?

The answer is that it is possible but not probable. The prohibition of "graven images" is unthinkable until the eighth century at the very earliest. So is the institution of the seventh-day sabbath. Even *after* that time the sabbath was related to the phases of the moon rather than the days of the week. If, therefore, the code we call the Ten Commandments was once a simpler code of briefer clauses, some of the clauses must have been quite different from the present ones. In that case, was it the same code?

It is time, however, for us to consider a further possibility. Just as the Pentateuch contains seven distinct codes of law, so it contains more than one decalogue.

4. The Primitive Decalogue

Once more we recall that in telling the traditional Sinai story we reached a point where we seemed to have lost the Ten Commandments, another and quite different decalogue having inscribed itself somehow on the Sinai tables of stone. Certainly it is after transmitting this code to Moses, and quite without interruption, that Yahweh says, " 'Write thou these words: for after the tenor of these words I have made a covenant with thee and with Israel.' And he was there with Yahweh forty days and forty nights; he did neither eat bread nor drink water. And he wrote upon the tables the words of the covenant, the ten words" (Exod. xxxiv: 27, 28).

It is not without interest that it was Goethe who first saw the significance of this more ancient code. He made it the subject of his inaugural disputation, insisting that it contained the original Ten Commandments. The Strassburg faculty was alarmed and would not publish so heretical a paper; Goethe therefore reworded it and had it published anonymously a few years later.

What was then a wild heresy is now the sedate consensus of a majority of scholars. The arrangement by Wellhausen is the one most generally adopted, although alternatives are possible and some scholars lengthen the code into twelve commandments. Certainly in Exodus xxxiv there *are* twelve rather than ten, but it is believed that this is due to the vicissitudes of the text and that originally what the passage contained was a decalogue.[4]

Here is the more primitive decalogue, often called the "Ritual Decalogue," as arranged by Wellhausen:

1. Thou shalt not worship any strange god.
2. Thou shalt not make unto thee molten gods.

[4] Series of ten are said to have been highly regarded by the ancients because, in recitation, they could be checked off on the digits of the two hands.

3. Thou shalt keep the feast of Unleavened Bread.
4. All the first born are mine.
5. Thou shalt keep the Feast of Weeks.
6. Thou shalt keep the Feast of Ingathering in the fall of the year.
7. Thou shalt not mingle leavened bread with the blood of my sacrifice.
8. Thou shalt not keep over until the morning the fat of my feast.
9. Thou shalt bring the best of the first-fruits of thy field to the house of Yahweh, thy God.
10. Thou shalt not seethe a kid in its mother's milk.

This decalogue, which is ritualistic throughout rather than moral, is undoubtedly the nucleus of the entire Covenant Code. The latter consists of the several chapters of the book of Exodus which contain older legislation, much of which, like the ritual decalogue here reproduced, was derived from Canaanite religion (Exod. xx, 23—xxiii: 33; plus the older nucleus, Exod. xxiv: 17-26).

It will be noted that the fourth commandment in this series requires the sacrifice of the first born and this means, as we shall later see, the first born of man as well as of animals. ("All that opens the womb is mine.") This, however, does not mean that the code is so ancient as to be pre-civilized, as the reader may be disposed to imagine, since infant sacrifice was only belatedly abolished in Canaanitish Israel. (It continued even until the third century B.C. in Canaanitish Carthage).

Was this the code, then, that was inscribed on the tables of stone? Again we shall have to say that it is very unlikely. This is not a code developed in the wilderness but relates to settled life and the pursuits of agriculture. So do the provisions of the passages of which this decalogue is the nucleus, the so-called Book of the Covenant. In fact, the Book of the Covenant is really Canaanite legislation.[5]

And thus, concerning decalogues written on tables of stone, we have exhausted the Scriptural possibilities. No decalogue known to us could have been given at Mount Sinai. We shall therefore, in a later chapter, turn to other

[5] See John M. Smith, *The Origin and History of Hebrew Law*. Chicago: University of Chicago Press, 1931, Chap. 2.

explanations of the stone tables; and we shall concern ourselves with the Ten Commandments in their true historical significance. First, however, we should notice one other code in the Pentateuch, and we should consider briefly the relationship of the Hebrew codes to other codes.

5. *The Code of Curses*

A codification different from the decalogues but providing a similar summary of concise admonitions is attributed to Moses in Deuteronomy xxvii. Instead of the formula, "Thou shalt not," we have "Cursed be he," and provision is made for the Levites to give ritual expression to the twelve excoriations, following each of which the people are to say "Amen."

"Cursed be the man that maketh a graven or molten image," the code begins, "an abomination unto Yahweh, the work of the hands of the craftsman, and setteth it up in secret. And all the people shall answer and say, Amen."

"Cursed be he that setteth light by his father or his mother," the series continues, thus echoing the Fifth Commandment as the first of the curses echoes the Second.

The third "Cursed" is for "he that removeth his neighbor's landmark," which suggests the coveting of a neighbor's field in the Tenth Commandment (Deuteronomy) which so often led to the surreptitious changing of boundaries.

The fourth, "Cursed be he that maketh the blind to wander out of the way," signifies compassion for the handicapped and retribution for callousness and cruelty. The fifth, "Cursed be he that wresteth the judgment of the stranger, fatherless and widow," is likewise protective of the defenseless and has some affinity with the Ninth Commandment, which forbids "false witness." In these two curses we are at the ethical level of the reason given for the sabbath in the Deuteronomic Fourth Commandment—a higher level than in the Exodus version or the rest of the Ten Commandments.

From the sixth curse to the ninth, however, the level abruptly descends, the subject being the prohibition of incest of various categories and of sodomy. The tenth is

a malediction upon secret assault; the eleventh excoriates
the purchase of an innocent person's assassination, and
the twelfth curses whoever will not conform to the code
that has just been uttered.

Here we see in a somewhat different form an arrangement of proscriptions thought to be particularly typical—
or perhaps in need of emphasis—drawn from the larger
code. As well as the significance attached to the selection
itself, it was doubtless looked upon as representing to some
extent the entire body of law that governed the society.

In the Pentateuch the larger codes as well as the decalogues are attributed to Moses, who received them from
the mouth of God. Their compilers, however, can scarcely
have intended that this should be understood literally,
even as to the part played by Moses. Moses was the symbol, the authority to whom it was possible to ascribe
whatever seemed to deserve his sanction. But the compilers must have known where the laws came from—at
least those that had recently been codified, and to this we
shall now give our attention.

6. The Mosaic Law and the Code of Hammurabi

The Code of the Babylonian empire-builder, King Hammurabi, was found in three broken pieces in the acropolis
of Susa (ancient Persepolis) by J. de Morgan in Decem-
ber, 1901, and January, 1902. Fitted together, the three
pieces form a huge shaft of black diorite, on the surface
of which are inscribed forty-nine columns of laws, total-
ing almost eight thousand words.

At the upper end of the column is a bas-relief, showing Hammurabi receiving the laws from the sun-god,
Shamesh, just as Moses is supposed to have received the
two tables of stone from the thunder-god, Yahweh. Evidently, the tradition that laws were transmitted to mortals in this supernatural way had ample precedent before
the time of Moses. However, the Babylonians must have
known that the laws Hammurabi had promulgated were
the same laws under which they had been living for some

time, only now they had been collected and unified and presented in a logical order.

Similarity between many sections of the Hammurabi Code and the Mosaic Law preserved in the Pentateuch has long been recognized. It is often so close that we must either suppose that considerable portions of the Mosaic Law are derived from the older Hammurabi Code or else that both are derived from a common source. It has been pointed out that during the Exile in Babylon (sixth and fifth centuries), when the Mosaic Law was being compiled, the priests of Israel had easy access to Babylonian legislation. This is quite true and the priests may have made use of this opportunity. But more recent knowledge leads us to see that it was hardly necessary. Hammurabi's Code had already reached Canaan, as also had other similar codes, before the invading Israelites began to settle there.

The former date for Hammurabi, c.2200 B.C., has had to be revised to c. 1800 B.C. This makes him more a part of the general cultural interactivity of this later period and we can be certain that not Babylon alone but the entire fertile crescent made its contributions to Hammurabi's Code. What eventually becomes law is first established as custom, and similar customs were being established (where conditions were similar) throughout this whole area.

It is not entirely easy to make an orderly comparison of Babylonian and Mosaic law. As one scholar complains, "Whatever view be taken of the similarities between the legislations, the greatest difficulty in asserting Babylonian influence is that the Israelitish law, as we know it, is a composite affair, of uncertain date, and combining new with old in a most perplexing manner. If we could be satisfied," he concludes, "that . . . any one stratum of [the Mosaic Laws] had preserved its original features, we might better institute a comparison."[6]

Nevertheless, comparisons can be made. It may be noted, for example, that in both cases the place of justice is the gate of the city; and that oaths must be made before God; furthermore, that warning is given in about the same terms against bribery, false witness, and sub-

[6] C. H. W. Johns, in HDB, extra vol., p. 608. (For list of abbreviations used in this book, see p. 135.)

terfuge to secure injustice. In both codes the woman is the possession of her husband and he is her lord or "baal"; dowry customs are the same, and so are the provisions relating to concubines, divorce and female slaves.

Both codes require the same punishment for false witness, i.e., that the one guilty of it shall suffer the exact fate he was preparing for the innocent; slander is punished in the same way; ordeal is prescribed for wives suspected of adultery; kidnapping is a capital offense; assaults upon a pregnant woman carry closely similar penalties.

These are only some of the comparisons. A complete outline would take many pages.[7] In an extended study, we should also have to expand the comparison somewhat by remembering that we now have Assyrian and Hittite codes from the same general period. These, too, in many ways are similar to Mosaic law but not as strikingly so as in the case of the Code of Hammurabi.

It is noteworthy that in Babylon, the *lex talionis* ("an eye for an eye, a tooth for a tooth," etc.) was insisted upon by the upper classes whereas financial compensation was provided for those of humbler station. Here we have the conservative aristocracy, clinging anxiously to custom even to its own hurt (as, in later times, aristocrats continued to fight duels). In Mosaic law, however, all Israelites (i.e. adult males who were heads of families: not women or slaves) were equal and all were aristocrats, and so the *lex talionis* prevailed to the exclusion of the more sensible provision of financial compensation.

The parallels between the Hammurabi Code and Mosaic law are found chiefly in the Book of the Covenant. Many scholars, as we have already noted, regard this "Book" as a Canaanite code which the Israelites adopted.[8] Certainly, the Israelites did more than merely "borrow" from the Canaanites; they absorbed the greater part of Canaanite culture. This culture had been created partly by the Canaanites themselves and was partly derived from Hit-

7 See John M. Powis Smith, *op. cit.* Contains translation of the Code of Hammurabi; also Assyrian and Hittite codes. The Code of Hammurabi is given in full in HDB, extra vol., pp. 599ff.
8 In addition to John M. Powis Smith, *op. cit.*, see Albert T. Olmstead, *History of Palestine and Syria to the Macedonian Conquest.* New York: Charles Scribner's Sons, 1931. Also Pfeiffer, *op. cit.*, Meek, *op. cit.*

tites, Amorites, Assyrians, Egyptians, Babylonians. But the Babylonian influence was apparently the greatest, and it was through the Canaanitish system chiefly that the influences of the Code of Hammurabi entered into Mosaic law.

7. *The Problem Reviewed: A New Standpoint*

In telling the traditional story of Mount Sinai, it will now once more and finally be recollected, we reached a point of complete frustration: on the basis of the record as it stood we were unable to tell what it was that was written on the tables of stone. Again, in following the narrative of the death of Moses, we were left with a sense of bafflement: why was his interment secret and the place of his burial a mystery? Since the traditional story did not answer these questions, we said we would leave it and turn to the story told by scholars.

This we have done and we still do not know what was inscribed on the tables of stone; nor have we solved the mystery of the death of Moses. Nevertheless, we have increased our understanding of the *actual* problem: a problem that traditional assumptions had obscured. Questions that were elusive have become clear to us. We know their real nature—as questions. The entire subject stands before us in a new light.

We see now that whatever happened at Mount Sinai, whether much or little—or even if nothing happened there at all—it is not important to the *true* story of the Ten Commandments. The Decalogue grew out of the life of the people, a landmark in their religious evolution. Though we cannot see him plainly through the mists of legend that bedim the face of history, we can recognize Moses as a great symbol: he was the Law-giver, not once and for all in the days of the wilderness but through all the centuries that followed, while Israel slowly learned that the Law of God is not the ritual of the altar but the call to righteousness.

It is in the context of this knowledge of a natural, social process, the results of which were at last momentous for morality and religion, that we shall now take up the meaning of the Ten Commandments.

CHAPTER FIVE

The Jealous God and the Chosen People

---

1. The Hidden Meaning of the First Two Commandments

The Decalogue was not intended for universal adoption; it was given to Israel to belong only to Israel. In appropriating it for wider use, this fact has been lost sight of and has led, in the case of the first two Commandments, to an unnoticed change of meaning. Let us begin, therefore, by recalling that the Decalogue is introduced by the announcement: "I am Yahweh, thy God, which brought thee out of the land of Egypt, out of the house of bondage." This is addressed to Israel and solely to Israel. Yahweh is Israel's national God; it was he who brought the Israelites out of Egypt.

Hence, when we come to the first of the Commandments, "Thou shalt have no other gods before me," we should understand that this means Israel. The Deuteronomist, in what is plainly an exposition of the first two Commandments, after forbidding the making of images, warns against reverence to "the sun, the moon and the stars, even all the host of heaven, [lest] thou be drawn away and worship them, and serve them, *which Yahweh thy God hath divided unto all the peoples under the whole heaven*" (Deut. iv: 19). The distinction could scarcely be clearer. The heavenly bodies have been appointed by Yahweh to be worshipped by the other peoples of the earth, but not by Israel. This implies, of course, that Yahweh has power over the other gods—it is he who has distributed them among the nations—but he does not dispute their right to be worshipped—except by Israel.

To make the restriction still clearer, the Deuteronomist continues: "[For] Yahweh hath taken you, and brought you forth out of the iron furnace, out of Egypt, to be unto him a people of inheritance, as at this day." What we have, then, in the First Commandment is the claim of Yahweh to be the national God of Israel, and no other God must be preferred before him.

This is not monotheism: the existence of other gods is not denied, but they are the gods of other peoples. This is not to say, however, that they can have no relation to Israel. The most probable translation of the Hebrew is "no other gods *before* me," not "*beside* me." Yahweh must have priority, but a subordinate place for other gods is not excluded. The actual words, literally translated from the Hebrew, are "Thou shalt have no other gods against my face." Exactly what this phrase means has been copiously discussed by scholars but remains debatable. The majority translate it "before me," and think it means not monotheism but henotheism—i.e., the belief in many gods but particular attachment to only one.

Nevertheless, in other passages—such as those quoted above from Deuteronomy—the Pentateuch seems to be forbidding any *worship* whatever of gods other than Yahweh. What this means is still not monotheism but monolatry: the belief in many gods but the worship of only one. But whichever way we interpret it the First Commandment is for Israel alone. Yahweh is the God of Israel.

Remembering that the first publication of the Decalogue, so far as is known, was in the seventh century B.C., we might date this conception of the relation of Yahweh to Israel to that period and expect that it was superseded in the centuries immediately following. But this was not the case. Revisers of Deuteronomy who lived late enough to know of the Jewish dispersion after the Exile (iv: 26-27) still adhere to this view of the relationship. And thus we must recognize how slow was the advance to monotheism.

In the case of the Second Commandment, too, it is Israel alone that is intended. Other peoples are not forbidden to make images; but Israel, after many centuries of image-worship, must be made to realize at last that *any* idol, even a representation of Yahweh himself, is sure to lead the people astray.

This, however, was in the seventh century. Until that time image-worship was not only not forbidden but was regarded as appropriate—even indispensable—to the worship of all the gods, including Yahweh. Unless we can believe in a minority tradition of imageless monotheism, stemming from Moses and perhaps Ikhnaton, as Freud did (and a very few scholars), we shall recognize that there was no protest against image worship for five centuries after the Exodus and very little against the worship of the gods of Canaan—or indeed of any other gods.

This we shall see in the following sections. But we may well begin by recognizing what the wide acceptance of the Decalogue has long concealed: that it was not a code intended for universal use and that it does not mean what we think it to mean. This we have discovered by looking a little more carefully than is usual at the first two Commandments; and we shall make the same discovery in several of the others.

2. Baal and Ashtart: Deities of Fertility

The word "Baal" is not the name of a particular god; it means "lord" and was applied to a great number of gods. To a Hebrew (or Canaanite) woman, her husband was a "baal": that is to say, he was her "lord" or master. Similarly, a goddess could be a "baalat," or mistress. Every locality had its "baal"—springs, wells, rivers, mountains, and inhabited places or cities. Nevertheless, the word Baal could be used inclusively to mean the god of fertility in all his manifestations.

Ashtart, too, the most ancient of the Canaanite divinities, could be a separate goddess in each geographical location. She could be the "Ashtart" of this place or of that, yet somehow in the end be just one goddess. In the later period, when the Scriptures were edited to severe Yahwistic standards, Ashtart was called Ashtoreth, indicating repugnance and contempt. The change of name was brought about by giving the word "Ashtart" the vowels of the word "bosheth," or "shameful thing," which was done also with such names as Melech, changing it to Molech. But Ashtart was not regarded as shameful until the later centuries had expelled her from Judaic worship.[1]

Such deities as Baal and Ashtart were indispensable to early agriculture. They were believed to ensure the fruitfulness of the ground, the multiplication of flocks and herds, the ripening of the vineyards and the entire livelihood of peoples who had settled on the soil. To suppose that desert tribes would move into Canaan and ignore Baal and Ashtart is the same thing as supposing that a citizen of a modern country would go abroad and totally ignore the lawful authority of the governments of foreign lands. Yahweh was the God of War who took his people into the Promised Land. But Yahweh had no power to bless the plough or cause the soil to yield its increase.[2] It was therefore inevitable that when Israelites settled in Canaan they would worship the deities of fertility who were the sovereign gods of the land.

To those who came to live in Canaan without ever having been in Egypt and who therefore presumably knew nothing of Moses (at that time) or of his God, Yahweh, the fertility cults could have offered not the slightest difficulty. Even to those who came later, after a sojourn in the wilderness, there could have been but little hesitation. Yahweh was the God of the confederation but Baal and Ashtart were the deities of the soil. It cannot be too greatly emphasized that at this time there was no objection whatever to sacrificing to whatever gods appeared to wield authority, and no one had thought of doing anything else. To plough the fields and ignore Baal was suicidal; to hope for a good lambing season and spurn the courts of Ashtart was the height of folly.

Moreover, as the Scriptures themselves allow us to perceive, the Hebrews had always worshipped local deities, as had all other Semites. The god who reveals himself to Jacob during his restless night at Luz announces that he

---

[1] עַשְׁתֹּרֶת (Ashtart), Gr ᾿Αστάρτη (Astartè); becomes עַשְׁתָּרֹת (Ashtoreth), Gr· ᾿Ασταρωθ , Astaroth.

[2] Even if he was in part a fertility god, he would not have in Canaan the powers he had had in Midian. Only after being in Canaan for some time would these powers accrue to him. But, irrespective of his symbols, he entered Canaan as a war god.

is the god of "that place," whereupon Jacob cries out that the place is Bethel (House of God), and erects a *matzebah* there—a stone pillar—in which the god (or "numen") can "reside." Only later is this god identified with Yahweh. For many centuries Bethel was the shrine of the local deity who revealed himself to Jacob when he slept there. In the Deuteronomic code, it may be noted, the use of *matzeboth* is strictly forbidden but it seemed entirely innocent to the writer of the story of Jacob.

It was often a *matzebah*, or rough unhewn stone pillar, that was the dwelling-place of Ashtart. Usually, a "cup" was hollowed out of the stone ("hewn" therefore to this extent) perhaps to receive blood, but sometimes this cavity was transferred to an adjacent altar. The exact significance of the *matzeboth* is difficult to discover, and discussion has been hindered by the reluctance of scholars to acknowledge its sexual symbolism. In any case, the *matzebah* is almost always surrounded by other pillars, definitely phallic symbols, and the actual nature of the cult is not in doubt.

The image of Baal was frequently that of a bull, the animal that more than all others signified insemination, quickening the earth's fecundity. Ashtart was represented as a woman, usually but not always nude, and often with a serpent coiled about her. In a typical figurine she stands with her hands holding her breasts outward, symbolizing the earth-mother anxious to feed her children; and with conspicuous genitalia, emphasizing the unbridled sexual license associated with the cult.

The worship of the Baals (Heb: Baalim) and Ashtart was not solely sexual, but sexuality was at its core. The ultimate basis was that of sympathetic magic: the soil must be encouraged to yield its increase and liturgical copulation would initiate the process and provide the incitement of a compelling example. This, however, was the inductive logic of more primitive worshippers than those of the Canaanitish Ashtart. While the magical principle was still retained as the *raison d'être* of the cult, the actual observances were those of methodical debauchment. Surrender to sensuality became the aim of a frenzied ritual; wild rhythms wore down restraint, lascivious pantomimes and uninhibited dances inflamed the appetites, until at last came the carnal abandonment which the prophets complained was to be found "in every high place and under every green tree."[3]

Among the temple attendants were *kedeshoth,* or women "dedicated" to the god or goddess, whose service was prostitution for the advantage of the temple treasury. There were also *kedeshim,* male prostitutes. There were "brothels" of the latter even in connection with the Temple of Yahweh at Jerusalem (II Kings, xxiii: 7). It was not uncommon, writes one scholar, for the earnings "of these male and female *hierodouloi* [to be brought] as a votive offering into the temple of Yahweh."[4]

It cannot be doubted that for several centuries Baal and Ashtart were supreme in Israel. The prevalence of the cult is amply attested by the number of theophorous names in which "baal" is incorporated. Eshbaal (man of Baal), Jerubbaal (he who fights for Baal),[5] Beeliada (Baal knows), may serve as examples. Later exegetes, after Baal worship had been suppressed, changed these names by substituting "bosheth" ("shameful thing") for Baal. (i.e., in pronunciation: there were no written vowels in Hebrew as yet.) Thus in II Samuel (ii: 8ff.) Ishbaal becomes Ishbosheth. On the other hand it is interesting that King Ahab, who was supposed to have abandoned the worship of Yahweh in favor of that of Baal, gave "Yahweh" names to his sons—as e.g., Ahaziah ('iah' = Yah).

With Ahab, however, it was not the worship of Baal that the Yahwist party objected to but the worship of a *foreign* baal, the Baal of Tyre. Queen Jezebel, daughter of the king of Tyre, had proposed to eliminate Yahweh-worship and substitute that of her own nation-state, the prosperous Phoenician city in the north. It was thus pa-

[3] For a novel based upon sound scholarship, describing the struggle between Yahweh and Baal and Ashtart, see *The Sinner Beloved* by Phillips Endecott Osgood. New York: America Press, 1956.
[4] E. Kautsch, in HDB, extra vol., p. 662. See also Adolphe Lods, *Israel from Its Beginnings to the Middle of the Eighth Century.* New York: Alfred A. Knopf, Inc., 1932, passim.; ERE, articles: Baal, Ashtart, etc.
[5] The opposite interpretation in Judg. vi: 32, is obviously forced and incorrect.

triotism that was the motive of Israelite resistance, not repugnance for the worship of Baal.

Here we can see, perhaps, what the true role of Yahweh in the early centuries must have been. First in Judah, then, after Solomon, in the north as well, Yahweh was the *national* God. Baal and Ashtart were the local deities of Canaan, engenderers of fruitfulness, fructifiers of the soil. And yet we must not over-simplify. The domains of Baal and Yahweh were at times identical. Just as there were many Baals, so, as the name came into common use, there were many Yahwehs. And from archeological findings we know that as late as the Persian period (fifth century B.C.) there was the cult of Anat-Yahu, the worship of Yahweh combined with that of a Syrian goddess not far removed from Ashtart!

Connected with the worship of Baal and Ashtart, and at times with that of Yahweh also, were the *asherim* or sacred poles. Originally these may have stood in place of trees, particularly the date palm, which was a widespread symbol of fertility. In Israel, as in Canaan previously, they were phallic pillars, generally of wood and very numerous. In temple use they were frequently carved into the semblance of the human form, with emphasis upon the reproductive organs, and it was an important provision of the cultus that there should always be temple women who wove hangings with which the posts were draped.[6]

Such was the worship of the Baals and Ashtart! Yet, we are not to suppose that it was nothing but the expression of crude sexuality. If we are to be objective we must keep in view that the sexual principle is pervasive of the whole of life; almost everything is either "he" or "she," masculine or feminine, and to the ancients this perception was nearer to the surface than it is with ourselves. Everything in life was polarized with either the one energy or the other, male or female, and thus the elaboration of a cult could carry it long distances from the raw realities with which it started.

Fertility is the central wonder of life, the great miracle that remains marvelous no matter how many times it is

6See ERE, vol. 10, p. 94a.

manifested; and this was the miracle, however much obscured by obscenity, that was commemorated by the Baal and Ashtart cults. It was a *physical* miracle; there was nothing in these cults—nor as yet in that of Yahweh—that was not materialistic. The spiritual was still in the future. Yet already there were premonitions of it. Ashtart was not only the primordial paramour; she was the nourisher, the life-giver, the great mother. Cruder, more gross, she was nonetheless the prototype of all the goddesses at length revered as Virgin-Mothers. She was the older sister of Ishtar and the cousin of Isis and Demeter. As her journeyings lengthen, she becomes less the insatiable Aphrodite (Venus) and more the *Mater Dolorosa,* the Mother of Sorrows. Actually she is that all along, says Professor Gilbert Murray, preëminent scholar in this field. "From the wanderings of Ishtar to those of Demeter . . . she is from the beginning the *Mater Dolorosa;* her heart is pierced not only by her own woes but by those of all her children. And it is important to realize—though the realization comes to the modern and uninitiated mind with a shock of repulsion—that on this adored figure of the Mother were heaped all possible passionate forms of man's love for woman. She is mother, sister, and bride; she is the eternal Virgin and the Beloved of innumerable lovers."[7]

As the worship of Yahweh, the national God, rose in esteem, largely perhaps because of the severe struggle after the ninth century for national survival, the fertility cults came more and more under the Yahwist party's condemnation. It was not Baal or Ashtart, said the prophet Hosea, who gave Israel corn and wine. It was—and always had been—Yahweh. Thus Yahweh absorbed more and more of the functions of the fertility gods but at the same time was changing in his own character.

By the time of the reforms of Josiah the Canaanite cults had become repugnant to a large enough fraction of the Judaic population to make feasible their systematic suppression. Moreover, national security required more and more reliance upon Yahweh. And so the time had come when Yahweh could be announced as a "jealous God," saying to his people, who had long sacrificed at many shrines, that they must henceforth sacrifice only at Jerusalem: and that above all they must give him unquestioned supremacy as their part in the Covenant: "Thou shalt have no other gods before me."

3. Molech and Infant Sacrifice

Even those who know the Bible fairly well are frequently shocked to learn that it tells of child sacrifice, still practiced on a large scale in the seventh century—which is to say a hundred years after Amos and Hosea, who inaugurated the age of the prophets. Sickening as it is to acknowledge it, we shall have to admit that even in this late period the practice did indeed prevail.

It had lasted for a long time. In the book of Judges we have the pathetic story of Jephthah's daughter, who came dancing with joy to meet her father as he returned triumphant from the wars. But foolishly Jephthah had vowed to Yahweh that he would sacrifice to him whatever came forth from the doors of his house when he returned from fighting the armies of Ammon. There was no possibility that Yahweh could release him from his ghastly vow, and so the unfortunate child was consumed in the flames of the altar. This story, be it noted, is told in approval of Jephthah's fidelity to his oath; and there is no shuddering at what is implied about the character of Yahweh (Judg. xi: 29-40).

When Jericho was rebuilt in the time of King Ahab, we are told that Hiel, the officer in charge, "laid the foundations thereof in Abiram, his firstborn, and set up the gates thereof in his youngest son Segub." This was fully in accordance with custom. No building was safe unless in its foundations—or in its walls—were the bones of a human sacrifice.[8]

The particular form of the immolation called "passing through the fire to Molech" was the sacrifice of the first-

---

[8] See George A. Barton, *Archeology and the Bible* (7th ed.), Philadelphia: American Sunday School Union, 1937, p. 169.

born as a burnt offering. Molech was not the name of the god to whom the sacrifice was made. Molech is merely the word Melech, or King, concealed by the trick which is by now, we may suppose, becoming somewhat familiar to us: the use by the later exegetes of the vowels of "bosheth," indicating "shameful thing." But it was Yahweh himself to whom the firstborn was sacrificed—Yahweh as King.[9]

The place where the children were sacrificed was called a "tophet," which, in Jerusalem, was just outside the walls in the valley of Hinnom. At Carthage, which was a Canaanite colony (Canaanite and Phoenician are the same), the "tophet" has been excavated by archeologists. It was more than three hundred yards long, a trench along the shore of the harbor, and we know that in emergencies, such as imminent invasion, large numbers of children were requisitioned from their families and incinerated there.

Besides Israel, Judah and Carthage, child sacrifice was practiced in Moab. A particularly arresting instance is the story of Mesha, King of Moab, who was attacked by a coalition of the Kings of Israel, Judah and Edom. When the battle was going hopelessly against him Mesha "took his eldest son that should have reigned in his stead and offered him for a burnt offering upon the wall" (II Kings, iii: 27). So immense was the preternatural power released by this sacrifice that Yahweh was helpless to contend with it and the Israelites fled before the Moabite god, Chemosh.

Here we begin to see the meaning of such sacrifices. The god himself has no freedom of choice if the sacrifice is great enough: he *must* respond and he is enabled to do so because the life immolated has activated a field of power which is now his to use for the end in view. It was when events were going badly and the survival of the nation was in doubt that child sacrifice increased in Judah. Yahweh would use the life-force with which he was thus endowed for the defense of Judah and the destruction of its enemies; and he would be *compelled* to act because he had been given what was most precious; there was nothing

9 See Barton, *op. cit.*, pp. 215ff.; Pfeiffer, *op. cit.*, p. 179; Arnold J. Toynbee, *An Historian's Approach to Religion*. New York: Oxford University Press, 1956, pp. 39ff.; HDB, extra vol., p. 619.

left to give except one's own life. This was the theory of infant sacrifice.

But the prophets denounced it. They boldly denied that sacrifice of any kind was efficacious or that Yahweh desired it. "Will Yahweh be pleased with thousands of rams, or with ten thousands of rivers of oil?" asks the prophet, Micah. Even the most fantastic, most prodigious sacrifices —*thousands* of rams, *rivers* of oil—do they have any effect upon Yahweh?

Then what *could* be effective? Micah was not sure. In condemning sacrifice he was partly rebuking his own fears, trying to silence the loudness of his doubts. The conflict— in its earlier stages—was not only *between* the prophets and the people: it was *within* the minds and hearts of the prophets themselves. To answer his question, sorely pressing in upon him now, Micah removes his last restraint and speaks out. "Shall I give my firstborn for my transgression, the fruit of my body for the sin of my soul?" And here we come to the crux of the matter—and to the beginning—*it is no more*—of civilized morality. Can a man atone for his wrongdoing by the voluntary loss of something that is precious to him? Not yet is the question asked as to whether a man *owns* his child and is entitled to *kill* him to gain divine favor. It is, as we have said, only the beginning of morality. But it is that.

What can sacrifice do—that is the question—for "the sin of the soul"? Even supreme sacrifice? And the prophet at last answers his own question: "He hath shown thee, O man, what is good: and what doth the Lord require of thee but to do justly, and to love mercy, and to walk humbly with thy God?"

But two generations later the children are still being incinerated at the Jerusalem "tophet." Then comes the discovery of "the Law" in the Temple. A priest had emerged at last, who, while not going as far as the prophets in their assertion of the supremacy of righteousness, had worked out a feasible charter of reform. When it is read to King Josiah, he rends his clothes. The reason Yahweh has abandoned his people is plain: they have utterly departed from his Law and forsaken his commandments. So Josiah decreed the changes that would bring the nation into conformity with the divine will. Among them was the prohibition of infant sacrifice. The Jerusalem "tophet" was "desecrated" so that "no man might make his son or his daughter to pass through the fire to Molech" (II Kings, xxiii: 10).

But it had lasted a long while. The date is 621! And Yahweh's moral stature is still far from high. If he is no longer the moody and tempestuous deity who at the slightest provocation will "break forth" upon his people, destroying them for ceremonial errors and mischances— yet unconcerned with moral wrong—he is still the "jealous God" who visits "the iniquity of the fathers upon the children." This is only one remove from absolving the fathers through the sacrifice of the children. But it is by such stages, as we have seen—and presently shall see more plainly—that the moral level of man and his gods has gradually risen.

4. The God of Israel and the Great Nations

When a small nation such as Judah is absorbed into a large empire—which in the case of Judah happened several times—its god is usually added to the imperial pantheon as a minor deity or else forsaken and forgotten. After all, the god of the little nation has been defeated; his humiliation is complete. Moreover, his land is now under the protection of the gods of the great empire. Of what use is he? Why should he be worshipped?

It is the distinction of Judah that this tendency was steadfastly resisted. Here we come, no doubt, to the value of the Covenant and of the belief that the Israelites were a "chosen people." Yahweh had made a promise. He would fulfil it in his own time and in his own way. Yahweh had extended his protection. There was none other in which Israel might trust.

But what could be said when the great empires subdued the little nation? Who was Yahweh to stand before Marduk? His people had been taken captive by the Babylonians. The Judeans, however, refused to be trapped in this dilemma. They solved it by extending Yahweh's power until it included Babylon. Not that Marduk, the god of Babylon, was denied; his existence was recognized and also his authority. But in international events affecting Judah this authority was subordinate to Yahweh's.

The inevitable effect of this was to move towards making Yahweh a universal God. But in that event what about his own people? Where was the protection he was to have afforded them? The answer given was that his own people had displeased him. They had followed after other gods. Or—as the prophets insisted—they had been unjust, oppressive, avaricious: they had sinned against man's duty to his neighbor: they had not followed righteousness. And so Yahweh had allowed his people to be dispossessed. Only, however, for the furtherance of his purpose. In the end, chastened and wholly obedient to his will, they would fulfil the mission to which he had predestined them; for they were to be to him "a kingdom of priests, and a holy nation."

This was the thinking of the Judean leaders from the times when the Deuteronomic Decalogue was promulgated, in the seventh century, to the time of the Priestly Code in the fifth and fourth. How should we evaluate it? One thing is clear: we should concern ourselves not only with what Yahweh *then was* but also with what he later became.[10] If he had not grown morally, the Judeans might as well have accepted Marduk, for Babylonian moral standards were higher than those of Judah at the time. Or later they might well have accepted Ahura Mazda or Zeus instead of being merely influenced by Persian thought and Hellenist philosophy.

The value of the "jealous God" of whom they were the "chosen people" was enhanced by that very intolerance which in one aspect we find repellent, but which in another we see to be the goad that drove Judeans toward the working out of a higher moral principle. An exclusive

10 When we speak of Yahweh as "growing," we obviously do not mean that he was an actual, supernatural person who underwent moral development. It is doubtless clear—but we emphasize it in any case—that we are talking of *the idea of God* as it grew during the history of a particular people. The temperamental deity of Sinai, or the Yahweh who demanded child sacrifice, had no substance whatever except as it was created in the minds of his people. All concepts of God, even the most primitive and pitiful, are attempts to approximate a sublime reality which is "the same yesterday, today and forever."

relationship to a God who was becoming the one and only God, and therefore the God of all mankind, carried heavy responsibilities. These in the end could only possibly be moral. And the Judeans would have to discover what they were.

But at the time the Decalogue was written this obligation was still in the future. Yahweh was the God of Israel, not of Israel's enemies. And Israel now was Judah; and the throne of God was Jerusalem. It was still some distance to the "God of all the earth," the Universal Lord and Heavenly Father.

5. The Shrines of Yahweh and the Temple at Jerusalem

In human society, the solution of one problem is usually the creation of another. This is what happened when the worship of Yahweh was centralized at Jerusalem. The aim of the reformers was to wipe out image worship, fertility rites, temple prostitution, the veneration of foreign gods, and infant sacrifice. In achieving this they made Jerusalem itself the object of idolatrous worship, the inviolable city of Yahweh which could not be destroyed.

The basis of the reforms was the oneness, not of God but of Yahweh. The distinction is important. In English, the famous *Shema* reads, "Hear, O Israel, the Lord our God is one Lord." This sounds like an affirmation of monotheism, and of course, the modern worshipper, for his own devotional purposes, is entitled to make it such. Historically, however, the meaning was quite different, as we can at once see by providing a literal translation: "Hear, O Israel, Yahweh our God is one Yahweh."[11] This means, not that Yahweh is the one and only God, but that the Yahwehs of the many shrines are non-existent, the only true Yahweh being the God of the Temple at Jerusalem.

Yet there was more than that. Yahweh worship had for many centuries been mingled with the cults of Baal and Ashtart. To the general reader of the Bible this may seem

[11]The reader has not forgotten, we trust, that the word which in the English Bible is rendered "LORD" (capitals), is the Hebrew word "Yahweh." See footnote. p 31.

a little startling but it has long been quite familiar to scholars. Some of the clues are in the language. As we have seen, the word "Baal" means "Lord," and the combination of the two names, "Baal" and "Yahweh," into "Baal-Yahweh," means only "Lord Yahweh." We have this very identification in the name, Bealiah (I Chron. xii: 5), which means "the Baal (Beal) is Yahweh (Iah)" or "Yahweh is the Lord." The Bible editors of a later period did what they could to disguise historical facts which had become embarrassing, but, necessarily, they left many indications of the truth. Today, however, we know, not only from the internal evidence of the Bible but from abundant archeological evidence, that the worship of Baal and Ashtart was continuous over many centuries, and that the worship of Yahweh was connected with it.

What also often happened was that the deity of a local "sacred place," such as Bethel, became identified with Yahweh, and this led inevitably to Yahweh worship being distributed at various shrines as though in every case he were a separate deity. Absolom, for instance, asks permission of King David, his father, to fulfil a vow in the presence of the Yahweh of Hebron. David sees nothing wrong with this request, even though he has himself brought Yahweh to Jerusalem (by bringing the Ark of the Covenant in which Yahweh traditionally resided). Clearly these are two different Yahwehs, although no doubt related (II Sam. xv: 7-9).

Perhaps we shall understand this situation better if we expand an earlier illustration and remember that the god of a particular sacred place was first of all just the "El" ("Strong One") of that place. Thus we have the "El" of Hebron. Then the word "Baal" comes more into use, so we speak of the "Baal" ("Lord") of Hebron. Presently Hebron becomes connected by revised tradition with an ancestral legend, say the visit of an Israelite patriarch of whom it has been asserted that his God was Yahweh. So now we speak of "the Yahweh of Hebron." This is one of the ways in which there arose a plurality of Yahwehs.

In innumerable other ways as well we find traces of what scholars call Israel's "polyjahvism," the worship of many Yahwehs. What the Deuteronomist wanted to bring about was therefore not monotheism but "monojahvism," the worship of only one Yahweh, the national God whose only true shrine was at Jerusalem. In this way the Jerusalem priesthood could control the cult completely, and as well as instituting much-needed reforms could greatly enhance its own prestige and enrich the central treasury.

This is what was behind the first two Commandments, establishing the national Yahweh as Israel's supreme God and prohibiting the making of images. In the Deuteronomic reform images of every kind were ruthlessly destroyed, but the Ark of the Covenant was allowed to remain. This was a serious defect, since it localized Yahweh in the Temple instead of permitting him to become the more spiritual God described by the prophets. That is why the later prophets, particularly Jeremiah, inveighed so strongly against the Temple and denounced its Ark of the Covenant. And that is why there was a constant controversy between the prophetic party and the party of the priests. Jerusalem, said the latter, was Yahweh's holy city and he would preserve it inviolate as long as he was worshipped as Judah's supreme God to whom alone his people offered sacrifice.

Not so, said the prophets. What Yahweh wants is righteousness. As for Jerusalem, it shall be destroyed. Its Temple shall become a heap of stones. Trees shall take root within its holy places. This was the controversy, and it will be seen from the nature of it how incomplete was the Deuteronomic reform. But as Pfeiffer has expressed it, the Deuteronomist "realized that an agreement between priests and prophets, representing the two types of religion . . . could only be effected through mutual concessions. Unfortunate as it may seem, no religious reformation based on the highest principles has ever achieved success without making important concessions to the religion of the masses; every important church represents such a compromise."[12]

---

[12] Pfeiffer, *op. cit.*, p. 180. An excellent discussion of the Deuteronomic reform will be found in William F. Badè's *Old Testament in the Light of Today*. Boston: Houghton Mifflin Company, 1915, Chap. 7, "The Monojahvism of Deuteronomy."

6. The Fertility Cults and the Forbidden Images

It is curious that the Primitive Decalogue forbids only "molten" images whereas the Second Commandment prohibits only "graven" ones. The first were of metal, generally bronze, and were cast in a foundry. The second were of carved wood, often overlaid with thin sheets of gold. Commentators have surmised that there may be some elusive meaning in the proscription of one kind of image and not of the other, but in the case of the Second Commandment both kinds seem to be covered by the detailed prohibition of "any likeness of anything that is in the heavens above, or in the earth beneath, or in the waters under the earth."

This interdict, most scholars agree, cannot be dated much earlier than the Deuteronomic reforms, since until that time images were widely used in Israel and it was not supposed that there was anything wrong with using them. It is true that King Hezekiah a century earlier had destroyed some of the "high places" and "cut down the asherah." It is also true and rather amazing that he had broken in pieces the bronze serpent (traditionally called the "brazen serpent") that Moses had made in the wilderness. But he had not forbidden every kind of image; there were still the "pillars" or *asherim* of Yahweh in the Temple, from which later he stripped off the gold coverings as part of the tribute he paid to Shalmanezer, the conquering king of Assyria (II Kings, xviii). There were doubtless also other images.

The truth is that in its older sources the Bible approves of images. Rachel carries away her father's teraphim, which he speaks of as his gods (doubtless his household gods, corresponding to the Roman penates) and nothing is said about idolatry (Gen. xxxi). David also has teraphim in his house, and it seems to be regarded as appropriate (I Sam. xix). Even the prophet Hosea, as late as the eighth century, laments the coming time when Israel will be bereft of king, prince and sacrifice, pillar (asherah), ephod and terraphim (Hos. iii: 4). These adjuncts to the worship of Yahweh were evidently regarded as essential.

Most conclusive of all, so far as Scripture is concerned, is the making of the bronze serpent by Moses. The destruction of this image by King Hezekiah was a bold break with tradition and must have had a powerful motive behind it. The Deuteronomic reform, carrying the prohibition of images much farther, must have included the same motive.

There were other images, of course, besides that of the serpent, but since we cannot inquire into them all let us give some attention to this one. It was important. The reason for its importance is not apparent in the Bible, but has been made plain by archeologists. The serpent was a fertility symbol. In typical plaques and statuettes of Ashtart the serpent is wound about her body or creeps out of the earth and coils itself around her thigh. Some commentators have tried to decry the sexual significance of this symbolism but it is too clear to be hidden. As pointed out by Albright in his description of some excavated figurines, "it will be noticed that in all these cases the serpent's head is directed toward the vulva of the goddess, a fact which proves conclusively that the serpent represents primarily the fecundizing *vis naturae,* while the goddess brings forth vegetation, symbolized by the flowers which she holds."[13]

In Semitic religion the serpent cult was unquestionably important. We have seen that the Levites were connected with it. We know from archeological evidence that snake-pits had something to do with Israelite religion. We know that the seraphim, later imagined as winged figures, were originally serpents. We know that incense was offered to the bronze serpent made by Moses down to the time that King Hezekiah destroyed it (II Kings, xviii: 4). We also know that from time immemorial the serpent has been connected in human imagination with sex symbolism, just as it is in the figurines of Ashtart.[14]

13 William F. Albright, *op. cit.*, p. 88. See also article, "Serpent Worship," ERE, vol. IX, pp. 399ff. See bibliography.
14 See article "Demons and Spirits (Hebrew)," ERE, vol. IV, p. 595.

To some scholars it has seemed likely that it was a serpent, perhaps originally a live one, that was kept in the Ark of the Covenant. What this "ark" was really like we now have no means of knowing, but if it was carried with the tribes during their wanderings in the wilderness it was probably a decorated box, dyed red, similar to those that we know were used much later by the Arabs.

Such an "ark" would be very suitable for the retention of a serpent but quite needless for the safe-keeping of tables of stone. Indeed, the latter, like the golden bulls attributed to Aaron, would almost certainly be prominently displayed.

What seems most likely is that the bronze serpent was substituted for the live serpent—quite possibly in the wilderness—and that this image became the representation in the south, as the golden bulls did in the north, of the Hebrew God, Yahweh.[15] As the scholar, R. H. Kennett reminds us, the bronze serpent and the ark are "the only two objects traditionally connected with the worship of Israel in the wilderness, of the existence of which there is any evidence in the period of the Kings."[16] Aaron, he goes on to say, is related to the golden bulls which were worshipped in the north, Moses with the bronze seraph (seraph = serpent) worshipped in the south. Both the bulls and the seraph were symbols of a fertility cult.

How, then, does it happen that the story as eventually told speaks of stone tables placed in the ark? The answer must be that before the bronze serpent was destroyed and the fertility cult abandoned Israel had moved more and more towards a religion of Law, and it was on stone tablets that law had traditionally been inscribed (as, for example, the Code of Hammurabi). Therefore, when the bronze serpent, the supreme symbol of the fertility cult, was destroyed, the tables of law were invented to take its place. They need never have actually been put in the ark; it was sufficient that the story appeared in the sacred literature.

But what of the ark? For a while it remained, as we have

[15] The ark could still be retained for a time, perhaps because it was less objectionable than the serpent, and possibly because custom had more firmly established it as a symbol of the presence of Yahweh.

[16] In ERE. vol. I, pp. 791ff.

already noted, a symbol of Yahweh in his Temple at Jerusalem. But presently it disappears from the story. There is no record of what happened to it. Perhaps it perished when Jerusalem fell in 586. But if so it is remarkable that there is no mention of it in the Scriptures. More likely a time came when the ark, too reminiscent of a now discarded cult, had to follow the bronze serpent into oblivion. Then a new "Ark of the Covenant," a work of literary imagination, could be produced during the Exile.[17] This is the Ark, idealized and fictional, of which we read in the Priestly Code and to a lesser extent in Deuteronomy.

This, at least, is one possible interpretation of how the transition was achieved. It is not necessary to insist upon the details. All we need to see is that in some such way the mind of Israel—or of its leaders—rebelled against the fertility cults and was determined to suppress them. To keep them suppressed it was decreed that there would never more be images. The national God was to be Israel's only God. And although sacrifice would still remain, and Yahweh would be worshipped with elaborate ritual, Judaic religion would be one of Law: from the reforms of Josiah would emerge the aspirations that led to a far higher level: the religion of the Torah.

7. The Commandment to Jonah

The exclusive relationship between Yahweh, the Jealous God, and his Chosen People, the Judeans, was more fervently asserted after the Exile than it had ever been before. Instead of discouraging the nationalism of the captives, the bitter experience of defeat and deportation made it strident and fanatical. This is always possible with a minority group that is tenacious of its own culture and confident of its eventual destiny. With the Judeans there was more than that: the meaning of their history was that Yahweh was leading them, even through anguish and humiliation, to the fulfilment of his purpose for them as a "holy nation."

---

[17] Many scholars doubt the historicity of the ark except as a "box" used in divination. But, irrespective of its other uses, it seems likely that it was originally a receptacle for an image.

Those who returned from the Exile (sixth and fifth centuries B.C.) after the Edict of Cyrus, the Persian, were therefore concerned as Judeans had never previously been to create a national life regulated in all respects by the exclusiveness of their religion. But since Yahweh, their own God, was now beginning to be seen as the supreme God, "the Ruler of all the Earth," it was necessary to define his attitude to other nations. This, as we have mentioned earlier, had already been done to a considerable extent by the prophets, but not upon the basis of a clear monotheism. Nor was it a clear monotheism even now, but Judean thought was moving strongly in that direction.

The dominant belief while Jerusalem was being rebuilt was that Yahweh was furious with other nations, especially those that had taken advantage of the deportation of Judeans to seize their undefended territory. Thus we have the denunciation of Edom by Obadiah, and the prediction of a coming "Day of the Lord" when such nations as Edom will be "consumed" and all the peoples of the heathen world will bite the dust.

This belief did not, however, go unchallenged. A more humane minority, the spiritual descendants of the great age of the prophets, were strongly repelled by the official creed and sometimes satirized it. The delightful book of Jonah is such a satire, its theme being the absurdity of believing that God is merciful only to Judeans: his lovingkindness is universal.

In effect Jonah receives a new Commandment—through being compelled to demonstrate the insufficiency of the older ones. He is to take Yahweh's word to the heathen, in fact to hated Nineveh, and warn of the impending hour of doom. Being perfectly certain that the doom will not arrive and that anyone who predicts it will appear ridiculous, Jonah quietly decides that he will get as far away from Nineveh as possible and sails from Joppa for the opposite end of the Mediterranean. Here the author of the story draws upon literary devices familiar in Oriental fiction and raises a great storm which the crew of the ship is convinced has descended upon them because God is angry with Jonah. Still, they (the despised heathen) want to spare him; but Jonah (the obdurate Judaist) refuses to be spared and at his own insistence is thrown overboard.

With sly drollery the satirist now creates a big fish which swallows Jonah and carries him back to where he started from. There the fish opens its mouth and Jonah is expelled, none the worse apparently for three days of ichthyic confinement, but gloomily aware at last that he will have to go to Nineveh.

At Nineveh he prophesies doom, as God requires, but the King and the people inconveniently repent, and God rescinds his edict. Jonah, intensely unhappy that God is responsive to the repentance of the heathen just as though they, too, were numbered with his people, drifts off into uneasy sleep while brooding outdoors and God provides a miraculous gourd which instantly springs up and shelters Jonah from the merciless heat of the sun. But the next day God finds a "worm" which destroys the roots of the gourd and it shrivels up, bringing from Jonah bitter lamentations and reproaches.

Then comes the moral of the story. "Doest thou well to be angry for the gourd?" God asks. "I do well to be angry even unto death," Jonah replies. Then, says God, if it is appropriate to be distressed by the loss of a gourd how much greater should be Jonah's distress at the thought of the destruction of Nineveh, involving the death not only of all the adults but of a hundred thousand infants "that cannot discern between their right hand and their left hand." And besides the children (a subtle touch) "much cattle"!

No one should look for fact in the story of Jonah; not only was there no "whale" but by the time of Jonah there was no Nineveh, either. The story is a moral satire, a parable inspired by the new and robust Jewish humanism.

What it means is that alongside the narrow concepts that still prevailed in the Judaic religion of the Yahweh of the Ten Commandments, there was emerging the wider view of a Universal God of all mankind, whose command was that man should prove his devotion to his Creator by the love that he showed to his fellow-man.

CHAPTER SIX

The Sacredness of Oaths, The Seventh Day, and Filial Duty

1. The Obscurity of the Third Commandment

"Thou shalt not take the name of Yahweh, thy God, in vain, for Yahweh will not hold him guiltless that taketh his name in vain"—this, the Third Commandment, has generally been interpreted as a prohibition of blasphemy. Blasphemy, in turn, has been understood as the use of God's name in curses, or as words spoken against God himself.

But there is no certainty whatever that it is blasphemy that the Commandment forbids. Literally translated the Hebrew text is as follows: "Thou shalt not lift up the name of Yahweh, thy God, unto nothing." What does "unto nothing" mean? Perhaps "to no purpose" or "for insufficient reason"; the name of Yahweh may thus be used only on solemn occasions, in worship or in the taking of oaths. It may not be used trivially. This comes close to blasphemy and yet is not quite the same thing. A curse can be solemn: it can also be sincere. It need not be intentionally the taking of Yahweh's name "unto nothing."

Some scholars have suggested that what is intended is the forbidding of the use of Yahweh's name in incantations or for divination. We know that even as late as the sect of the Dead Sea Scrolls (last centuries B.C. and part of the first century A.D.) there was a concern lest holy names be used in sorcery. In a well-known passage in the first book of Samuel (xxviii) we read of wizards and "people with familiar spirits" who can call forth the dead from

Sheol by the use of the correct formula. It is implicit in such beliefs that the one whose name is invoked, even though he be a god, is bound to respond, so great is the potency of names.

Another suggestion relates to the ritual practice of calling upon the name of Yahweh when bringing a sacrifice. The Third Commandment is thus regarded as having the same meaning as the commandment in the older ritual code (Exod. xxxiv): "None shall appear before me empty." What this amounts to is that there shall be no worship without sacrifice. Thus the preference for prayer over sacrifice—which was quite old, being very evident in Document J—is explicitly condemned.

Unfortunately for the possibility of making a clear choice, any of these interpretations may be right. Those who feel that it is blasphemy that is being forbidden can offer the testimony of the passage in Leviticus xxiv, in which "the son of an Israelitish woman, whose father was an Egyptian," got into a quarrel with a full-blooded Israelite, and, when it seemed that he was being outfought, "blasphemed the Name and cursed," presumably to bring the potency released by such an imprecation on to his side of the battle.

According to the story, which is obviously intended for later use as a legal precedent, the blasphemer is brought before Moses, who, however, is uncertain as to what shall be the penalty. The trial is therefore recessed until Moses can discover the will of Yahweh. One of the difficulties is evidently that one might curse Yahweh secretly, in which case, since the sin was not known except to Yahweh, no penalty could be imposed except by Yahweh directly. The question was, then: Should the same conditions apply when the curse was overheard by others—namely, public blasphemy? The decision is that secret cursing shall be left to Yahweh (there seemed to be no option) but that public blasphemers shall be stoned to death.

Against this background we may ask whether the Third Commandment is not addressed to the former case— secret blasphemy—since it warns that "Yahweh will not hold him guiltless that taketh his name in vain." In other words, the secret blasphemer may escape punishment at the hands of fellow-mortals who are unaware of his sin, but he cannot escape the punishment imposed by God.

2. Its Most Probable Meaning

We cannot be certain that any of the foregoing explanations of the Third Commandment is correct—or even that it applied at all to blasphemy. We do know that the name of Yahweh was protected by provisions which are not found in other religions. Islam has no penalty for blasphemy itself but treats it as a form of heresy. If one holds the name of God in low regard it is evidence that one does not believe the doctrine.

In classical Greece blasphemy was a crime against the state, since it might call down the wrath of the offended god—who would not discriminate between the guilty individual and his community. In Rome there was no law against blasphemy. Disparagement of the gods was taken to be rebellion against the political authority of which the gods were symbols. The concept of blasphemy as a sin would have seemed irrelevant to the Greeks and Romans: what they were concerned with was crimes against the state.

Only in the religion of Israel—and therefore also in Christianity—is blasphemy a sin. This brings us to the special character of the name of Yahweh, which, etymologically, as we have seen, is so fraught with contradictory possibilities that it can be made the basis of almost any theory. If in using the name Yahweh the post-Exilic Judeans were chiefly reminded of the primitive god of Sinai-Midian, whose image was the "brazen serpent" made by Moses, or the golden bulls worshiped in the northern kingdom, they may have wanted to suppress it in favor of the word "Adonai" or "Lord," which conveyed their loftier, later view of God. This, rather than an extreme sense of sanctity, may have been the original reason for forbidding the use of Yahweh's name.

Certainly by the third century B.C., when utterance of the name of Yahweh was first—supposedly—officially forbidden, Judaic religion was much too highly developed to be intimidated by the primitive taboos against vocalizing the names of deities. There was no more natural reason for it than there would have been if the Greeks had suppressed the name of Zeus, or the Romans that of Jupiter, or the Babylonians, Persians and Egyptians their usual names for God. The, impression one gets is very strong that the name of Yahweh was *intended to be suppressed;* just as history was being rewritten to new standards so were theology and ritual. It is therefore possible, especially if the Decalogue was considerably revised in the last rescensions of the Pentateuch, that the Third Commandment reflects to some extent the wish that the name of Yahweh might pass out of sight, except in the esoteric comprehension of the scribes.

These are some explanations, all possible but none provable, of the ambiguous Third Commandment. Such suggestions deserve to be considered, and must be, if the reader is to understand the problem. Most probable, however, is a rather simpler explanation. When an oath was sworn in the name of Yahweh, it had to be fulfilled under all circumstances. Otherwise Yahweh's name had been taken "for nothing" or "in vain." Moreover, the oath was used not only to solemnize a contract but in the taking of testimony, a practice based upon the Code of Hammurabi (§§ 20, 103, etc. *cf.* Exod. xxii: 7, 8, 9, 11). A man accused of a crime for which witnesses could not be produced was taken "before Yahweh," there to declare on oath his guilt or innocence. If he perjured himself he might escape the prescribed punishment. But not the penalty imposed by Yahweh. Men might be deceived, but Yahweh "will not hold him guiltless that taketh his name in vain."

The reader thus may take his choice between these explanations. The last given is not actually more certain than the others—but somewhat more probable.

3. Seventh Day Observance: A Late Development

Traditionally the seventh day sabbath is believed to go back either "to the beginning" when God rested after six days of creation or else to the time of Moses, at Mount Sinai, when the Ten Commandments were inscribed on tables of stone.

The first derivation is only possible if we substitute the mythological for the historical. The second, as we have seen, involves believing in tables of stone which probably never existed; but even if they did it is certain that they did not contain the Fourth Commandment. Of this Commandment, as we have several times noted, the Bible contains two different versions, each of which in style and content belongs to the particular period when the Scripture which contains it was compiled.

We may ask, however, whether Sabbath observance may not have been well established long before the Decalogue was written. The answer is that there was indeed "sabbath" observance, but it was not of the *seventh day* Sabbath. It was not related to the days of the week but to the phases of the moon. The Israelites did not take it with them into Canaan; they found it when they arrived there. To some of the prophets it was a "heathen" observance which they condemned and excoriated. "New moon and sabbath," says Isaiah, "and the calling of assemblies—I cannot endure iniquity and solemn assembly. Your new moons and your appointed feasts my soul hates" (Isa. i: 13). In the same vein, Hosea says in the name of Yahweh, "I will put an end to all her mirth, her feasts, her new moons, her sabbaths" (Hos. ii: 11). Evidently, to win its way to ethical approval, such as that of the Deuteronomist, the Canaanitish Sabbath had to change and evolve and become something very different.

That there could have been a seventh day Sabbath in the wilderness, when traditionally it is supposed to have been instituted, is of course impossible. "The Sabbath," writes Professor Pfeiffer, "is inconceivable among the nomads of the desert: either they are raiders, and then every day is a Sabbath when they are not on a foray, when no Sabbath would be observed, or they are shepherds and their work cannot be interrupted one day in seven, as in farm work."[1]

1 Pfeiffer, *op. cit.*, p. 231.

The shepherd's work, says Dr. Lods in a more explicit description, "which must be done every day, consists in feeding and watering his flocks."[2] It also consisted in protecting his flocks from thieves and from beasts of prey. If the shepherd had observed the Sabbath the thief would have observed his opportunity, and so would the lurking animal marauders.

No scholar, however, regards the seventh day Sabbath as having been established among nomads in the wilderness. The word *shabbath* comes almost certainly from the Babylonian *shabattu,* which denoted the feast of the full moon. The other regularly occurring feast was that of the new moon. So when we read in the Bible of "new moons and sabbaths" what it means is feasts of the new moon and of the full moon. These were taken over by the Canaanites from the Babylonians, who took them, no doubt, from the Sumerians; and it well may be that the nomad Hebrews had observances which, without being the same, were somewhat parallel. None of them were days of rest except to the extent that work stopped during the feasting.

The new moon and full moon "sabbaths" were related, as was all Canaanite religion, to the fertility cults and had the same significance for the Hebrews. That is why the prophets declaimed against them. The seventh day Sabbath, on the other hand, is definitely a Judaic development. It probably emerged—we do not know how—under the influence of the eighth-century prophets, the emphasis being first on a day of rest. This was the Deuteronomic Sabbath. Later, during the Exile in Babylon, when the older observances, including sacrifice and the Temple ritual, were interrupted, it doubtless took on additional significance as represented in the version in the Priestly Code. But what clues do we have which might indicate its origin?

The Babylonians, as we know, abstained from work on certain days not because they were sacred but because they were "unlucky." Work begun on such a day would invite misadventures and might cause an injury to the worker. It was unwise to work on days that experience had proved to be ill-omened. The unlucky days are be-

[2] Lods, *op. cit.*, p. 438.

lieved to have been the seventh, fourteenth, twenty-first and twenty-eighth of the two months, Elul II and Marcheswan. Perhaps "unlucky" days were also found in other months. The same superstition may have existed in Canaan, borrowed from the Babylonians. But if this was the practice the Judeans took over they certainly transformed it. Instead of the seventh day Sabbath being an unlucky day it became a day of thanksgiving and rest, a spiritual and humanitarian observance.

Of other sabbaths we may note that the Christian or "Lord's Day" Sabbath is derived from the Jewish practice as modified by Mithraic ritual (which moved it from the seventh day of the week to the first) during the early Christian centuries. The Muslim Sabbath is derived from both the Jewish and the Christian but the period of abstinence from work lasts only while services are being conducted at the mosque. It occurs on Fridays. There is a Buddhist Sabbath, the Uposatha, which is the day of the new moon and of the full moon and of the eighth day following each. It owes nothing to the Jewish or Christian Sabbaths.

There is much more that we would like to know of the origin of the Judaic Sabbath, but its history has many blank spaces that we can only fill in with inferences. To complete our outline, however, the importance of the Sabbath was greatly increased by the dispersion of the Jews and the rise of the synagogue. With the Temple remote and no opportunity for sacrifice, the congregations in distant lands depended more and more upon Sabbath observance as the nurture of their religion and the opportunity to study their Law.

4. The Purpose of the Sabbath: Two Views

A comparison of the text of the Fourth Commandment as it appears in Deuteronomy and in Exodus has already been made (Chapter Four). What now remains to be noted is the religious significance of the divergence between the two: the earlier version (Deuteronomy) gives the basis of the Sabbath as humanitarian, the later version (Exodus) as one of piety.

There is some indication that a day of rest may have been observed by the privileged classes for some time before it was extended to the populace in general, though the argument, admittedly, is rather tenuous. On the Babylonian seventh day (*u-hul-gallum* or "evil" day: not *sabbath*), we are told that "the shepherd of the great tribes shall not eat salted meat cooked over the embers, he shall not change his body-clothing, he shall not be clothed in white, he shall not offer a sacrifice. The king shall not ride in a chariot, he shall not talk victoriously. The seer shall not make declaration with regard to a sacred place. A physician shall not touch a sick man. It is not suitable to make a wish. . . . In the night the King shall bring his offering into the presence of Merodach and Ishtar, he shall make a sacrifice. The raising of his hand in prayer is acceptable to the god."[3]

It seems possible that all the references here are to the ruling and professional classes; *u-hul-gallum* may not have been observed by the common people. If with the passage of time the emphasis came to be less on the "unluckiness" of the day and more on its opportunity for rest, the seventh day in Canaan may have become a rest day for the privileged classes. In this case, the Deuteronomist is extending its benefits to all members of the community, including the slaves. The Sabbath is intended, he says, "that thy manservant and thy maidservant may rest as well as thou."

For this democratic widening of the rest day privilege he gives an admonitory reason: "Thou shalt remember that thou wast a servant in the land of Egypt, and Yahweh, thy God, brought thee out thence by a mighty hand and by a stretched-out arm: therefore Yahweh, thy God, commanded thee to keep the Sabbath."

Here, clearly, the purpose is one of human welfare, and it is evident that Jesus was a Deuteronomist in expressing his view that "the Sabbath was made for man, and not man for the Sabbath." Was there a controversy on this subject between Deuteronomists and sacerdotalists, even in the time of Jesus? From what we know of the debates current in this disputatious period, it is entirely likely.

[3] See ERE, vol. X, p. 890.

In the Priestly Code, composed a century or a century and a half later than Deuteronomy, the basis of the Sabbath is that Yahweh rested on the seventh day after his six days of creation. "Wherefore Yahweh blessed the sabbath day and hallowed it." The purpose has thus been changed from one of human welfare to one of pious observance. The day upon which God rested is a day set apart; none of his people must do any work on this holy day: work would profane it.

What has happened is that during the Exile the Priestly party has gained control and the emphasis of the prophets has been largely lost. This change is seen not only in the new basis given for observing the Sabbath but in the total outlook of the Jewish leaders, which outlook they were determined to impose upon the Judean community. In this, after the restoration of Jerusalem, they largely succeeded—but never completely. The prophetic party was not dead, nor had its teaching been deleted from the Scriptures. Only "so far" could the Priestly party go—and perhaps only "so far" did it want to go. But unfortunately, under Ezra and Nehemiah, who were courageous and high-minded leaders but nevertheless narrow in their viewpoint, the Sabbath lost much of its earlier quiet beneficence and became a ritual observance, rigorously enforced.

The priestly basis given for Sabbath observance—that God rested on this day—is, of course, mythical. Just as the world was not created in six days, so was there no seventh day of divine rest. Indeed, the very notion of God resting is an anthropomorphism that theology—even traditional theology—is bound to reject: either that or do what it can to explain it away.

It is unfortunate that this version of the Fourth Commandment, rather than the Deuteronomic, is the one that has passed into general use. Irrespective, however, of the choice of version and the unsolved questions of its origin, the Jewish Sabbath, in its centuries of observance, has deepened greatly in religious meaning. This meaning is most concisely expressed, perhaps, in the second stanza of a beautiful Jewish hymn that is sung at the table on Friday evening:

Treasure of heart for the broken people,
Gift of new soul for the souls distrest,
Soother of sighs for the prisoned spirit—
The Sabbath is rest.
This day is for Israel light and rejoicing,
A Sabbath of rest.

5. *"Honor Thy Father and Thy Mother"*

As commonly interpreted the Fifth Commandment is perfectly clear: parents should be respected by their children. In its historical context, however, its meaning is far from plain. The parents were not equal: the mother, as the father's wife, was his possession. The father could have more than one wife: was the mother to be honored but not the stepmother?

If the father died his first born son at one time inherited his wives as concubines, with the exception of his own mother. Daughters were possessions that could be sold into concubinage or slavery. In this case a daughter had no right of protest; she must obey. But in what sense would she "honor" the father who for his own enrichment had abandoned her to degradation?

What of the children born of slaves? They might honor their father from whom they derived their patrilineal dignity, but could they honor his female bond-servant who lacked the status of a wife?

So many are the difficulties of reconciling this Commandment with the social conditions that obtained in the Israel to which it was given that many scholars have decided that it relates to the ancestor worship which is known to have had so large a place in early Hebrew religion rather than to the contemporary family. More likely, however, is Badè's suggestion that the Commandment is addressed only to adult male Israelites and refers to the aged parents of sons who had formed their own households.[4] Since they were now beyond parental control these adult sons were no longer obliged to obey their

---

4 W. F. Badè, *op. cit.,* p. 114. A similar Islamic commandment seems to bear out this interpretation: "Be kind to your parents whether one or both of them attain to old age beside thee" (Qur'ran; sura xvii; 24).

parents as formerly; they might even show them disrespect, as Reuben did when he ravished a concubine owned by Jacob, his father. For this, however, Reuben suffered when the time came for his father to give him his blessing. And this may be a clue to the meaning of the Fifth Commandment.

What we read is (Exodus): "Honor thy father and thy mother: *that thy days may be long in the land* which Yahweh, thy God, giveth thee." A dishonored father could curse his son, and so devastating was the effect of such a curse, as the Israelites viewed it, that the son's life might be cut off. Curses had important (magical) effects, no matter who uttered them. And of all curses the curse of a father was the most potent. Under this construction the Fifth Commandment was therefore a warning. "You may be outside your father's household," it says, "and no longer under his command; but you are not beyond the range of his curses. Be careful, then, to honor him, and his wife, your mother, lest he curse you and your days be ended."

In Deuteronomy, besides the connection of the Fifth Commandment with long life, we have the clause "that it may go well with thee," which fits in perfectly with this interpretation. Besides the foreshortening of life a father's curse could bring misfortune, but his blessing was assurance that it would "go well with thee." There is thus, to quote Badè, a "sinister as well as an auspicious significance" to this Commandment.

Such then was the Fifth Commandment's likeliest meaning in its own historical context. But time has sufficed to give it a simpler and more beneficent meaning. We are to honor our parents because they gave us life and shelter, and—it is to be hoped—kindness and love. Modern psychology, however, would caution us that the matter is not that simple. Parent-child relationships are full of pitfalls. If a child insists upon honoring a dishonorable parent it may cause emotional aberration. If a child is too intensely devoted to a parent it may warp him so that he is unfitted for making a home of his own—or even unable to cope with normal life at all. So that it is best to see in this Commandment a reasonable reminder rather than an edict; and even to remember that in the view of Jesus all the people were "his mother, his sisters and his brethren" (Mark, iii; 31-35). This means that a true religion widens kinship until it includes the entire human family. Yet in seeking the larger we must not neglect the lesser: and this is the enduring value of the Fifth Commandment.

CHAPTER SEVEN

The Four Criminal Laws and the Sin of Coveting

---

1. The Old Testament Meaning of Murder and Theft

From the Sixth to the Ninth Commandments we are dealing with an ancient criminal code. Here there can be no doubt that we go back to the time of Moses and considerably beyond. All societies, once they had emerged from the primitive, forbade murder, adultery, theft and false testimony. But to these terms they gave their own definitions, relative to the stage to which they had advanced. Israel is no exception. These four Commandments were unquestionably in effect in the earliest nomadic days, but as the tribes settled down to agriculture and slowly became a nation there evolved from the new conditions a new social environment and the old laws took on new meanings.

When, therefore, the Decalogue was promulgated in the seventh century, these four Commandments were understood in the cultural context then prevailing, which was certainly far advanced from the one prevailing in the wilderness. On the other hand it was not by any means the cultural context with which we are ourselves familiar. Just as a considerable distance had been traversed, so there was a considerable distance still to go—as there still is: modern society can scarcely claim to be the end of the journey.

In discussing these Commandments it will be convenient to take the Sixth and the Eighth together, and then, in a separate section, to return to the Seventh. The Sixth Commandment does not say in Hebrew, "Thou shalt not kill," but "Thou shalt not murder." What murder meant originally was the slaying of a fellow-clansman. It was often a duty to kill a man of another clan. The practical basis was that the loss of a man was the loss of a soldier, and thus one's own clan was weakened in comparison with its rivals. But the practical basis acquired "mystical" significance. The loss of a clansman was a crime against his ancestors. It was thus a sacred obligation to retaliate by killing a member of the offending clan.

In the earlier days little distinction was made between murder and manslaughter, the deliberate and the accidental killing of another man. Even in the Covenant Code which is the context of the Decalogue, blood-revenge for manslaughter was still permitted, but amelioration was provided through "cities of refuge" where the accidental slayer could grasp one of the "horns of the altar," there to remain until he could be brought before the judges.

It is not to be thought, however, that blood-revenge applied only to current slayings. It could be entailed for many generations. The later Arabs allowed it to cease in the fifth; but previously the murder of a clansman might impose the duty of avenging him upon children's children for an indefinite duration.

Killing in war, including the annihilation of entire populations, men, women and children, was not murder. As we know from the Bible, such massacres were believed to have been decreed by Yahweh. To spare the enemy, even to have mercy upon a single individual, brought a curse upon the entire community. Here it should be noted that the modern world has little to boast; there is still mass annihilation even if there is no longer ritual slaughter.

While death was the penalty for murder if a free man was killed, financial compensation was enough in the case of a slave. If a man murdered his own slave there was no penalty at all, since it was considered that he had merely destroyed his own property. Children also, until (in the case of males) they were grown and had established their own households, were counted property, and so infant sacrifice was not murder but a sacred act of immolation.

When we come to theft we see once more that we are

dealing with crime only if it is committed against another member of one's own community. It was Yahweh himself, according to the Bible story, who told the Israelites to "borrow" from the Egyptians their "jewels of silver, jewels of gold, and their raiment" with no intention of returning them. Between Yahweh and his people there was no covenant at this stage (i.e., at the time the story was written: ninth century B.C.) involving morality. Yahweh was bound to his people by a ritual contract; they were his "clients" whom he was bound to prosper if they maintained his worship and his sacrifices. Theft, therefore, like murder, was not a crime unless it was perpetrated within the tribes.

But by the time of the prophets a moral sense had emerged which incited them to cry out against the expropriation of foreigners. Aliens who lived in Israel should be dealt with justly; they had the same inherent rights as Israelites themselves. Something of this we see also in the legislation which surrounds (and thus defines) the Ten Commandments. The protection of some of Israel's laws is to be given to "the stranger which is within thy gates." Yet, not of all. A Hebrew debtor must have his debts cancelled at the end of seven years; but of an alien, "thou mayest exact it."

Only gradually has religion climbed towards the ethical, and only gradually did it do so in Israel. Nowhere do we see this more plainly than in the original meaning of the Sixth and Eighth Commandments.[1]

2. The Definition of Adultery

In the modern world adultery is "voluntary sexual intercourse on the part of a married person with any person of the opposite sex other than the lawful spouse."[2] But the Seventh Commandment had quite a different meaning. It was not adultery if a concubine or a female slave was violated. In these cases the offender made

[1]For this and the following sections, see particularly John M. Powis Smith, *op. cit.* On general subject of Judaic criminal code, see articles, "Crime nd Punishment (Jewish)" in the encyclopedias (ERE , JEnc, EBi, etc.).
[2]*New Century Dictionary.*

reparation by a cash settlement with the woman's owner. But in the case of adultery the penalty was death.

What, then, was adultery? It was sexual intercourse between a legal wife who had been acquired by purchase and a man who was not her spouse. Even a betrothed bride who was not yet actually wedded to the man who had bought her was counted his wife for legal purposes; it was therefore adultery, and thus a capital offence, if any other man seduced her *after the purchase price had been paid*. Until then, however, it was a much less serious matter, one that could be financially adjusted through the civil code (Exod. xxii: 16). So that what we are dealing with is not moral chastity but the rights of property. Through these rights the wife was bought out of her own family into her husband's, where her legal status was that of his chattel. As such, she became the vehicle of transmission of her husband's family heritage, and her inviolability was the assurance of legitimate descent. Only in her case, therefore, was an extra-marital union called adultery.

That women were counted property there can be no doubt. Even Yahweh himself so counts them when he tells King David that in punishment for his carnal sins he will "take thy wives before thine eyes and give them to thy neighbor." How the wives feel about this proceeding is given not the slightest thought. According to early traditions even adultery was permissible if it saved the husband (and owner) of a woman from harm. Abraham is twice said to have passed his wife off as his sister so that she could be seized for another man's harem without the other man feeling that he must first get rid of Abraham. Apparently Yahweh approves of this proceeding since he brings afflictions upon the other men—not Abraham— which not only cause them to restore Sarah to her husband with all possible haste but induce them to load Abraham with presents as well!

The relationships of Hebrew men with other women were no concern of their wives. The marriage laws were written by and for men. The standards, of course, were those of polygamy. And more broadly they were the sexual standards of the time. What these were may be better understood when we observe how detailed were the prohibitions against incest. It was doubtless essential that the code be made precise under polygamous conditions where the head of the family, in addition to having children by more than one wife, might also have them from concubines and slaves.

Then there was the confusing institution of levirate marriage, which required sexual union with a deceased brother's widow if she had not borne him a son. While it was a crime punishable by death for a man to have carnal relationships with his brother's wife while his brother was still living, it was a sacred obligation upon him to do so if his brother were dead. In fact, as well as maintaining his own marriage it was his duty to raise up a "first born son" to his brother, so that his brother's line would not die out.

The list of sexual sins that occurred often enough to need codification is far from edifying. We must remember, however, that in all these matters we are dealing with a society that only recently had given up (if it had entirely done so) the fertility cults with their ritualistic orgies. Nor were conditions worse in Israel than in adjacent countries. Even in Babylon, which was more enlightened in some of its legislation, the code was no better in the rights accorded to women.

In this respect it is interesting to see in the Hittite Code how little morality there is in what are called (by editors) its laws against unchastity. In Law 191 we read: "If a free man picks up now this one, now that one [meaning women], now in this country, now in that country, there shall be no punishment. If both [women] live in one place and he know [have carnal knowledge of] them, it is a capital crime." So long as there is no propinquity and the two women are unaware of their "husband's" philanderings, no harm is done! But if the women live close together and know themselves as rivals, the man must suffer death for it. Could law be more capricious or chastity more opportunist?

The Hebrew Code is more advanced than that, although it is often surprising to see how closely similar to each other the codes of western Asia remained even over long periods. It is a curious fact that in all of them the laws regulating commerce are more equitable than those regulating human relationships. Yet it would be misleading to suppose that in the latter we see reflected everything that was important in the social conditions of the time. If, for instance, women were without rights, they were certainly not without influence. Legally a wife might be a chattel, but to her husband she could be a beloved spouse.

The better side of human nature was not absent because it was not featured in the laws. And this we should remember in studying the laws of any earlier period, including the legal background of the Seventh Commandment.

3. Purveyors of False Testimony

No laws are more ancient than those forbidding false witness. In the Code of Hammurabi it is the subject of the first enactment: "If a man accuse a man, and charge him with murder, but cannot convict him, the accuser shall be put to death" (§1). The meaning is not that a man shall suffer for an accusation made in good faith, which he is not able to sustain before the judges, but that a deliberately false accusation shall bring upon the man who makes it the same penalty that would have been inflicted upon the accused if he had been proved guilty.

In the fourth law of the Code we have a similarly precise construction of equity in the provision that if a man "offer [false] testimony concerning grain or money he shall himself bear the penalty imposed in that case" (§4).

In the Ninth Commandment, as in the Covenant Code of which it is a part, the penalty is not stated. What we have is: "Thou shalt not bear false witness against thy neighbor" (Ninth Commandment), "Thou shalt not take up a false report" (Exod. xxiii, 1), "Thou shalt take no gift [bribe], for a gift blindeth them that have sight and perverteth the cause of the righteous" (Exod. xxiii: 8). These are prohibitions rather than laws.

There are similar prohibitions—"Thou shalt not wrest the judgment of thy poor in his cause. Keep thee far from a false matter" (Exod. xxiii: 6, 7)—which also are not accompanied by stated penalties. But from the Deuteronomic Code we discover that punishment was upon the same basis as the Code of Hammurabi: "If an unrighteous witness rise up against any man to testify against him of wrong doing" he shall be brought before the judges, who shall "make diligent inquisition," and if it be determined that "the witness be a false witness, and hath testified falsely against his brother, then shall ye do unto him as he had thought to do unto his brother . . . and thine eye shall not pity: life shall go for life, eye for eye, tooth for tooth, hand for hand, foot for foot" (Deut. xix: 16-21).

One reason for the great importance attached to truthful testimony is considered to be the reduction in the availability of witnesses owing to the probability that only men were allowed to testify. Since women held no negotiable property they could have paid no fines; and since they were themselves the property of their husbands or fathers (sometimes of other male kinsfolk) with the obligation of obedience, their testimony could be presumed to be constrained. In short, they would have to say what their male proprietors told them to say, and no penalty could be imposed upon them for this since it was their legal duty to obey.

Slaves, both male and female, bore the same limitations. Only men, therefore, could be witnesses, whether false or true. Although this is the opinion of many authorities it may well be doubted whether quite so sweeping an exclusion of women—or even of slaves—from the opportunity to testify was ever feasible. There is no doubt, however, that in Israel law was a matter between men.

In any case the requirement of veracity, not only in preferring criminal charges but in all matters that could damage another person's interests or reputation, has been upheld since the dawn of civilization. Like the three other Commandments that express prohibitions elaborated in the criminal codes, it is not Hebrew but universal. Murder, adultery, theft and false witness, although variously defined at different times and in different places, have been crimes carrying severe penalties ever since man began to make laws.

4. The "Evil Eye" or Coveting?

The terms of the Commandment against coveting presuppose settlement upon the land, which was one of the earliest reasons given for the improbability of the Decalogue going back to Moses. The neighbor's house (not tent) must not be coveted; and in Deuteronomy, his field (not grazing space). In the wilderness where there were neither houses nor fields (in fact, no ownership of real estate at all), there would have been no reason for this Commandment, and as an anticipation of problems to be encountered later it is quite incredible. However, as we have seen, the evidence against a Mosaic date for the Decalogue (except that Commandments Six to Nine could go back much further) is conclusive without this argument.

Because it seems to deal with inner consciousness rather than outward deeds, this Commandment has frequently been held to be more "spiritual" than the others. Not only must a neighbor's property not be *stolen,* but the very *desire* to possess it must not be entertained. That this is the meaning of the Commandment has, however, been contested. The Hebrew word for "covet" can be construed to mean "acquire." Eerdmans maintains that it means "to appropriate that which has no individual owner."[3] To support his argument, he quotes from the Covenant Code: "Neither shall any man *covet*[4] thy land when thou goest up to appear before Yahweh, thy God, three times in the year" (Exod. xxxiv: 24). He interprets this passage as meaning that during prolonged absence a man's land may be said to be vacated and can legally be "coveted" or appropriated. Since it is known that sophistries of this sort were much employed at the time, the argument is plausible except that it applies only to land. What of the neighbor's wife, his house, his slaves, his animals? Could these also be seized?

Or did the Commandment in an earlier form mention only land? The verb "covet" could be rather wide in its

[3] Translated in Badè, *op. cit.*, p. 127.
[4] The word translated "desire" in the pertinent passage in English Bibles is the word for "covet" in Hebrew.

meaning, indicating not only desire but also the connivance which so easily follows from desire, in which case we have the idea of contriving opportunities to gain possession, perhaps within the letter of the law, of the neighbor's wife and slaves as well as his animals and land. These categories could therefore be added later, and to contemporaries there might be no ambiguity.

Still further objection to the conventional interpretation is made by scholars who contend that coveting was similar to the casting of a spell or to "the evil eye," which bewitched the persons or property enviously admired and thus eventually led to the possession of them through the power of sorcery.[5] All this is possible. But it is also possible that what the Commandment means is what it seems to mean: that evil deeds begin with evil desires, that there would be no theft without avarice, no murder without hate, and that no evil of any kind could ever take substance if it had not first of all been entertained in thought.

It is doubtless true that at the time this Commandment took its final form there was "much taking of others' land even by violence," and that these aggressions were legally justified by "casuistical juggling,"[6] but nonetheless the desire had to precede the deeds that embodied it. If, moreover, it was circumvention of the intent of the law that led to the addition of the comprehensive clause, "nor anything that is thy neighbor's," it does not alter the fact that the result was an all-inclusive condemnation of coveting.

It seems natural, therefore, to regard the Tenth and last Commandment as a transition from the externalism of edict and prohibition to the internal and more clearly moral world of attitude and motive. This, after all, had been the emphasis of the prophets.

[5]See Edward W. Lane, *The Manners and Customs of the Modern Egyptians*. New York: E. P. Dutton & Co., Inc. (Everyman's Library), 1923, Chap. 11.
[6]ERE, vol. IV, p. 516.

5. *Results of the Study: A Summary*

As we have now many times seen, the Ten Commandments could not have been given by God to Moses and were never inscribed on tables of stone. Overwhelming evidence assigns them to a period at least six hundred years later. Even as a briefer decalogue they could not have existed in Mosaic times. In the case of the version made public by King Josiah, in 621 B.C., when he promulgated the book of the Law found in the Temple, the language and ideas are distinctively contemporary—seventh century and Deuteronomic. The Exodus version is later: Exilic, a revision by the writers of the Priestly Code.

There had been an earlier, primitive decalogue, entirely ritualistic, which a former tradition had associated with tables of stone. This, although retained in the sacred writings, the Ten Commandments had superseded. Some of the Commandments existed individually long before the time of Moses, since they are found in all ancient criminal codes. Others were composed when the Decalogue was compiled.

As a whole the Ten Commandments reflect the advance of Israelite religion to the point that was reached just before the Exile. They show the influence of the prophets but are below their ethical standard. A considerable distance had been traversed, but there was still far to go.

Finally, the Decalogue became a symbol of Israel's long and arduous pilgrimage, a sacred token of the great transition from a religion of superstition and sacrifice to one of righteousness and law.

CONCLUSION

The Modern Meaning of the Ten Commandments

The esteem in which the Ten Commandments have been held has long been due not to their contents but to their place in religious history. To the traditionalist they were given by God to Moses and hence are sacred. To those who reject their supernatural origin they form an ancient moral code which is presumed to have high value because it has attracted so much veneration.

But whether traditionalist or otherwise, whoever really studies the Ten Commandments as a guide to ethical behavior is bound to find them insufficient. Their provisions are too few and too elementary. Civilized societies have long since taken many of them for granted as the most obvious components of their criminal codes. What we need for our ethical guidance is not so much the prohibition of murder, which most of us are not likely to commit, as some indications of the positive virtues. Kindness, generosity, sympathy, courage, love—these are the ethical values that we look for in a high moral code.

Even the ritual provisions of the Decalogue fall below modern standards. How many of us now believe in a "Jealous God" who is bound by covenant to one particular people—the Yahweh of the First Commandment? He has long since been superseded, both for Jews and Christians, by the God who is the Father of all mankind, the Universal Lord.

Does this mean then that the Decalogue is depleted of religious value, that it has meaning only for the past, that the time has come to discard it? Not in the least!

It remains a great religious symbol, signifying the turning point when a people whose spiritual inheritance is shared with all of us began to forsake their false beliefs for faith in the God of moral law.

Let us consider for a moment what this means. We have studied Israel's religion in its earlier phases: barbaric customs, temple prostitution, degrading forms of worship, infant sacrifice. We learned how massacres were ordered —so the people thought—by Yahweh, Israel's God. We saw that Yahweh was regarded as a cruel despot, jealous, capricious, not knowing evil from good.

But this was not peculiar to Israel's religion. In its earlier phases religion has always been like that. All the gods at first were cruel: they were made in the image of their worshippers and could only grow, morally, as their worshippers grew. What the reader must recognize, therefore, is that what he has been following is for the most part a *typical* religious history. His own ancestors engaged in the same degrading practices as did the Israelites. It is not where Israel *started* that has ultimate significance—but where she *arrived*.

Religious progress has come stage by stage. There has been no way of hurrying it. That is how it came in Israel. The horrors of infant sacrifice gave way to the butchery of animals. The lamb was substituted for the first born son, as in the story told of Abraham and Isaac. Then, finally, the ritual slaughter ended altogether. In Israel the Temple gave way to the synagogue. God was seen in a new light. He was invoked not by splashing blood upon some sacred stone but in the insights of his prophets and the meaning of his Law.

That is what, today, the Ten Commandments signify: the turning-point in a long struggle to liberate religion from debasing custom and false belief; the difficult ascent from a low moral level toward a high one. And since from Israel's struggle the civilization of the West has drawn so much, making it a part of its own religious heritage, it is appropriate that we continue to exalt its greatest symbol, and this, to the modern mind, should be the meaning of the Ten Commandments.

APPENDIX A

The Two Versions of the Decalogue Precisely Compared

Translation:

The American Revised Standard Version, amended to more literal accuracy.

PREFACE:	Exodus xx:	I am Yahweh, your God, who brought you up out of the land of Egypt, out of the house of bondage (bondsmen).
	Deuteronomy v:	The same.
ONE:	Exodus:	You shall have no other gods before (or beside) me. (*Literally,* You shall have no other gods against my face.)
	Deuteronomy:	The same.
TWO:	Exodus:	You shall not make (for) yourself a graven image, or any likeness of anything that is in the heavens above, or that is on the earth beneath, or that is in the water under the earth; you shall not bow down to them or serve them; for I, Yahweh, your God, am a jealous God, visiting the iniquity of the fathers upon the children to the third and

fourth generation of those who hate me, but showing steadfast benevolence to thousands of those who love me and keep my commandments.

Deuteronomy: The same.

THREE: Exodus: You shall not take the name of Yahweh, your God, in vain, for Yahweh will not hold him guiltless who takes his name in vain. (*Literally*, You shall not hold up the name of Yahweh, your God, for nothing, etc.)

Deuteronomy: The same.

FOUR: Exodus: *Remember* the sabbath day, to keep it holy. Six days you shall labor, and do all your work; but the seventh day is a sabbath to Yahweh, your God; in it you shall not do any work: you, or your son, or your daughter, your manservant, or your maidservant, or your cattle, or the sojourner who is within your gates; *for in six days Yahweh made heaven and earth, the sea, and all that is in them, and rested the seventh day; therefore Yahweh blessed the sabbath day and hallowed it.*

Deuteronomy: *Observe* the sabbath day, to keep it holy, *as Yahweh, your God, commanded you.* Six days shall you labor and do all your work; but the seventh day is a sabbath to Yahweh, your God; in it you shall not do any work: you, or your son, or your daughter, *or* your manservant, or your maidservant, *or your ox, or your ass, or any of* your cattle, or the sojourner who is within your gates; *that your manservant and your maidservant may rest as well as you. You shall remember that you were a servant (slave) in the land of Egypt, and Yahweh, your God, brought you out thence with a mighty hand and an outstretched arm; therefore, Yahweh, your God, commanded you to keep the sabbath day.*

FIVE: Exodus:

Honor your father and your mother, that your days may be long in the land which Yahweh, your God, gives you.

Deuteronomy:

Honor your father and your mother, *as Yahweh your God commanded you,* that your days may be *prolonged, and that it may go well with you* in the land which Yahweh, your God, gives you.

SIX: Exodus:

You shall do no murder. (*Literally,* Murder not.)

Deuteronomy:

The same.

SEVEN: Exodus:

You shall not commit adultery.

Deuteronomy:

Nor shall you commit adultery. (Virtually the same.)

EIGHT: Exodus:

You shall not steal.

Deuteronomy:

Virtually the same.

NINE: Exodus:

You shall not bear false witness against your neighbor.

Deuteronomy:

Virtually the same.

TEN: Exodus: You shall not covet your neighbor's *house;* you shall not covet your neighbor's *wife,* or his manservant, or his maidservant, *or* his ox, or his ass, or anything that is your neighbor's.

Deuteronomy: Neither shall you covet your neighbor's *wife;* and you shall not *desire* your neighbor's *house, his field,* or his manservant, or his maidservant, his ox, or his ass, or anything that is your neighbor's.

APPENDIX B

The Decalogue and Moral Codes

of Other Great Religions

Resemblances between the Judaic codes of Law and the Code of Hammurabi (Babylonian, 1700 B.C.) have been noted in the text. It is certain that the former, which were under development from about the eleventh to the fifth centuries B.C., are in part derived from the latter, perhaps through the Canaanite codes. But no decalogue is known, Babylonian or other, that closely resembles the Ten Commandments. Individual provisions (Commandments Six to Nine) are to be found, though not in this precise form, in all ancient criminal codes. But as a compilation the Decalogue appears to be unique.

Nearest to it, in the opinion of many scholars, is the famous Chapter 125 of the Egyptian Book of the Dead, the guidebook for the souls of the departed which charted their way, if they were fortunate, into the abodes of blessedness. In this chapter, the deceased stands before the "great God, lord of Righteousness," and makes his "confession"—actually denials that he has committed the sins named in the ritual. Among these denials are the following: "I have not slighted God. I have not slain. I have not commanded to slay. I have not committed fornication or impurity. I have not stolen. I have not spoken falsehood." Which, as we immediately see, do resemble some of the Commandments.

But there are many others: "I have not been an eavesdropper. I have not been a gossip. I have not made mischief in matters not my own. I have not been deaf to words of truth. I have not multiplied words in speaking. I have not railed against the King." These bear no resemblance to the Ten Commandments. One of the clauses, "I have not done harm to the doer of evil," is on a considerably higher level than the Ten Commandments and reminds us of the words of Jesus, "Do good unto them that hate you."[1]

[1] Article, "Ethics and Morality (Egyptian)," in ERE, vol. V, p. 478.

Although, as we have noted, there is no Babylonian equivalent of the Decalogue there are cuneiform tablets inscribed with condensed precepts which are broadly comparable to the Decalogue. One of them reads:

"Slander not, but speak kindness;
Speak not evil, but show good will;
Whoso slanders and speaks evil,
Unto him will Shamash requite it.
Open not wide thy mouth, guard thy lips;
If thou art provoked, speak not at once;
If thou speakest hastily, thou shalt afterwards have
    to atone therefor;
Soothe rather thy spirit with silence.
Offer daily unto thy god
Sacrifice, prayer, and incense most meet for the Deity,
Before thy god shalt thou have a heart of purity;
It is this that is due to the deity."[2]

When we come to Buddhist morality we are in a different and more mystical world than the Judaic; still, the famous "Four Noble Truths," the fourth of which defines the "Eightfold Path," is similar to the Ten Commandments in the veneration it has attracted:

"The Four Noble Truths"
I. Existence is unhappiness.
II. Unhappiness is caused by selfish craving.
III. Selfish craving can be destroyed.
IV. It can be destroyed by following the eight-fold path,
    whose steps are:
    1. Right understanding
    2. Right purpose [or aspiration]
    3. Right speech
    4. Right conduct
    5. Right vocation
    6. Right effort
    7. Right alertness
    8. Right concentration

To be meaningful to a Western mind this code needs considerable interpretation, which is impossible here; we must be content to cite it as occupying a Buddhist status comparable

[2] Alfred Jeremias, *The Old Testament in the Light of the Ancient East.* New York: G. P. Putnam's Sons, 1916.

to that of the Decalogue for Jews and Christians.[3]

Although Islam has no decalogue it has a series of commandments which are probably based upon the Hebrew Decalogue; the following is an abridgement (numerals supplied):

1. Set not up another god with Allah. Thy Lord hath ordained that thou shalt worship none but him.
2. Be kind to your parents, whether one or both of them attain to old age beside thee. Speak to them in gracious words.
3. To thy kinsman render his due, and also to the poor and the wayfarer.
4. Kill not your children for fear of poverty. Beware, for killing them is a great wickedness.
5. Withhold yourselves from adultery, for it is an abomination.
6. Slay not anyone whom God hath forbidden you to slay, except in a just cause.
7. Touch not the substance of the orphan, except in a righteous way, until he attains years of strength.
8. Perform your covenants; verily, a covenant will be investigated.
9. Give full measure, and weigh with an equal balance.
10. Follow not that of which thou hast no knowledge.
11. Walk not proudly in the earth; thou shalt not reach the mountains in height.
12. Avoid the evil, hateful in the sight of your Lord.[4]

Further comparisons would only be possible in a more extended study. We shall merely mention in conclusion that the Decalogue has often been compared—and sometimes, because of its less benign spirit, rather sharply contrasted—with the Beatitudes, nine in number, with which, in Matthew's Gospel, Jesus commences the Sermon on the Mount. But the Beatitudes are not a moral code, or really comparable to the Decalogue. They congratulate or "esteem fortunate" (Gr. makarios)[5] certain classes of people who, because of their unusual virtue or present state of deprivation will later receive a recompense.

[3]For a brief and readable treatment, see Edwin A. Burtt (ed.) *The Teachings of the Compassionate Buddha.* New York: The New American Library, 1955.
[4]*Qur'ran;* sura xvii, 23-40.
[5]From μακαρίζω = to call happy.

List of Abbreviations Used in This Book

EBi —*Encyclopedia Biblica*
EBr —*Encyclopaedia Britannica*
ERE —*Encyclopedia of Religion and Ethics*
HDB—*Dictionary of the Bible*—Hastings
ICC —*International Critical Commentary*
JEnc —*Jewish Encyclopedia*

BIBLIOGRAPHY

Bibles

HEBREW:

Haupt, P. (ed.). *The Sacred Books of the Old Testament.* 8 vols. Leipzig: J. C. Hinrichs, 1896-1904.

Kittel, Rudolf (ed.). *Biblia Hebraica.* 2 vols. New York: G. E. Stechert & Co., 1913; Stuttgart, 1937.

ENGLISH:

Revised Version, 1884 (RV), mostly quoted in this book; *American Revised Standard Version,* 1952 (RSV).

The Old Testament

Driver, Samuel R. *An Introduction to the Literature of the Old Testament* (rev. ed.), New York: Charles Scribner's Sons, 1901. The classical work in English. Needs supplementation to be brought down to date.

Frazer, James G. *Folklore in the Old Testament.* London: Macmillan & Company, Ltd., 1919.

Gray, George B. *A Critical Introduction to the Old Testament.* New York: Charles Scribner's Sons, 1913; London: 1919. Concise.

The International Critical Commentary on the Holy Scriptures of the Old and New Testaments. New York: Charles Scribner's Sons, since 1895. Various authors.

Kittel, Rudolph. *Geschichte des Volkes Israel.* 2 vols. Stuttgart-Gotha: F. A. Perthes, 1923-25.

Lofthouse, W. F. *The Making of the Old Testament.* London: 1915.

Moore, George F. *The Literature of the Old Testament.* New York: Henry Holt & Co., 1913; London: Williams & Norgate, 1913.

Oesterley, William O. E. and Theodore H. Robinson. *An Introduction to the Books of the Old Testament*. New York: The Macmillan Company, 1934; London: The Society for Promoting Christian Knowledge, 1934.

Pfeiffer, Robert H. *Introduction to the Old Testament*. New York: Harper & Brothers, 1941 and 1948. The best modern introduction, with extensive bibliography.

Sellin, Ernst. *Introduction to the Old Testament*. New York: George H. Doran Co., 1923.

Wellhausen, Julius. *Die Composition des Hexateuchs* etc. Berlin: G. Reimer, 1899.
> "Israel," in EBr, 1909.
> *Prolegomena zür Geschichte Israels*. Berlin: 1905.

Historical

Badè, William F. *The Old Testament in the Light of Today*. Boston: Houghton Mifflin Company, 1915. A very readable modern analysis.

Bertholet, Alfred. *A History of Hebrew Civilization*. New York: Brentano, 1926; London: G. G. Harrap & Co. Ltd., 1926.

Burney, Charles F. *Israel's Settlement in Canaan* (2nd ed.). New York: Oxford University Press, 1919.

Kent, Charles F. *History of the Hebrew People*. 2 vols. New York: Charles Scribner's Sons, 1904.

Lods, Adolphe. *Israel from Its Beginnings to the Middle of the Eighth Century*. New York: Alfred A. Knopf, Inc., 1932; London: K. Paul, Trench, Trubner & Co. Ltd., 1932.

Meek, Theophile J. *Hebrew Origins*. New York and London: Harper & Brothers, 1936. A standard interpretation.

Oesterley, William O. E. and Theodore H. Robinson. *A History of Israel*. 2 vols. Oxford: The Clarendon Press, 1932.

Olmstead, Albert T. *History of Palestine and Syria to the Macedonian Conquest*. New York: Charles Scribner's Sons, 1931.

Archeological

Albright, William F. *The Archeology of Palestine and the Bible*. New York: Fleming H. Revell Company, 1935.
> *From the Stone Age to Christianity*. Baltimore: Johns Hopkins, 1940.

Barton, George A. *Archeology and the Bible* (7th ed.). Philadelphia: American Sunday School Union, 1937.

Breasted, James H. *The Dawn of Conscience.* New York: Charles Scribner's Sons, 1934.

Burrows, Millar. *What Mean These Stones?* New Haven: American Schools of Oriental Research, 1941.

Kenyon, Frederick. *The Bible and Archeology.* New York: Harper & Brothers, 1940; London: G. G. Harrap & Co. Ltd., 1940.

Periodicals:
   American Journal of Archeology
   The Biblical Archeologist
   Bulletin of the American Schools of Oriental Research.

Religion of Israel

Albright, William F. *Archeology and the Religion of Israel.* Baltimore: Johns Hopkins, 1942.

Leslie, Elmer A. *Old Testament Religion in the Light of Its Canaanite Background.* New York: Abingdon Press, 1936.

Löhr, Max. *A History of Religion in the Old Testament.* New York: Charles Scribner's Sons, 1936.

Oesterley, William O. E. and Theodore H. Robinson. *Hebrew Religion: Its Origin and Development* (2nd rev. ed.). New York: The Macmillan Company, 1937.

Peters, John P. *The Religion of the Hebrews.* Boston: Ginn & Co., 1914.

Smith, Henry P. *The Religion of Israel.* New York: Charles Scribner's Sons, 1914.

Smith, William Robertson. *Lectures on the Religion of the Semites.* Edinburgh: A. & C. Black, 1889; 3rd ed., with Introduction and notes by S. A. Cook, London: A. & C. Black Ltd., 1927; New York: The Macmillan Company, 1927.

Law and Morals

Cook, Stanley A. *The Laws of Moses and the Code of Hammurabi.* New York: The Macmillan Company, 1903; London: A. & C. Black, 1903.

Smith, John M. Powis. *The Origin and History of Hebrew Law.* Chicago: University of Chicago Press, 1931.

———. *The Moral Life of the Hebrews.* Chicago: University of Chicago Press, 1923.

Miscellaneous

Campbell, R. A. *Phallic Worship*. St. Louis, 1888.

Cutner, Herbert. *A Short History of Sex-Worship*. London: C. A. Watts & Co. Ltd., 1940.

Erman, Adolf. *The Literature of the Ancient Egyptians*. New York: E. P. Dutton & Co., Inc., London: Methuen & Co. Ltd., 1927.

Frazer, James G. *The Golden Bough* (3rd. ed.). London: Macmillan & Company, Ltd., 1951.

Freud, Sigmund. *Moses and Monotheism*. New York: Alfred A. Knopf, Inc., 1939.

Gray, George B. *Sacrifice in the Old Testament; Its Theory and Practice*. Oxford: The Clarendon Press, 1925.

Scott, George R. *Phallic Worship*. London: T. Werner Laurie Ltd., 1941.

Wake, Charles S. *Serpent Worship*. London: G. Redway, 1888.

Encyclopedias

The encyclopedias listed below have articles on almost all areas of Biblical criticism but are not always down to date.

Encyclopedia of Religion and Ethics (ERE), 12 vols. & Index.

Jewish Encyclopedia (JEnc), 12 vols.

Catholic Encyclopedia (CE), 16 vols.

Encyclopedia Biblica (EBi), 4 vols.

Dictionary of the Bible—Hastings (HDB), 5 vols. (the one-volume edition is of limited value to the serious student).

Encyclopaedia Britannica (EBr), 14th edition.

Atlas

Westminster Historical Atlas to the Bible. Philadelphia: The Westminster Press, 1945. Excellent maps and informative articles.

INDEX

140

*The Greatest Challenge to Christian Dogma Since
Darwin's Theory of Evolution*

THE MEANING OF
THE DEAD SEA SCROLLS
by A. Powell Davies

Signet Key #Ks339—35c

In this outstandingly popular and readable bestseller,
Dr. Davies answers the questions that thousands of people
are asking:

1. How were the Scrolls discovered?
2. When were they written?
3. How were they deciphered?
4. Who were the Essenes?
5. What is the relationship between the new
   knowledge derived from the Scrolls and the
   teachings of Jesus? Is this discovery a gain or
   a loss for religion?
6. What are the various interpretations of the
   Scrolls?
7. What will their effect on religion and science be
   in the future?

Universal critical acclaim was bestowed on THE MEAN-
ING OF THE DEAD SEA SCROLLS in such glowing terms as:

"A fascinating study of a fascinating subject."
—*Worcester Gazette*

"What a 35 cents worth! I found it to be an immensely
readable book, telling in simple terms the true facts
about one of the most amazing discoveries of our
time." —Malcolm Bayley, *Vice-President of
National Life and Casualty Company*

"Dr. A. Powell Davies . . . tells the story of the series of
discoveries since 1947 in a book that should bring
their light to every person who wants to know more
about them." —*Washington Post & Times Herald*

"A book fascinating to anyone interested in Judaeo-
Christian culture." —*San Francisco News*